Praxis II Education of Young Children (5024)

How to *Think Like a Test Maker*™ and pass the Praxis 5024 using effective test prep, relevant practice questions, proven strategies, and constructed response practice.

KATHLEEN JASPER

Kathleen Jasper LLC
Estero, FL 33928
http://www.kathleenjasper.com | info@KathleenJasper.com

Praxis II Education of Young Children (5024): How to *Think Like a Test Maker*™ and pass the Praxis 5024 using effective test prep, relevant practice questions, proven strategies, and constructed response practice.

Printed in the United States of America
ISBN: 9798332981852

I'm Kathleen Jasper, and for the last decade, I've been helping prospective teachers and school leaders pass their certification exams and get the positions they want in education. To date, I've helped over 80,000 educators through their certification journeys.

I've had many positions in public education. I started off as a substitute teacher and went through the certification process you are going through right now. I was hired as a high school reading and biology teacher, and a couple of years later had the opportunity to work in curriculum at the district office. Finally, I became a high school assistant principal.

I left public education to start my own company, Kathleen Jasper LLC, and now I write study guides, conduct online courses, create content, and more to help you pass your exams and land your desired position.

I am thrilled you're here. Thank you for taking the time to review my content and purchase my products. It means the world to me to help educators all over the country.

Would you mind leaving a review?

Did you purchase this book on Amazon? If so, I would be thrilled if you would leave an unbiased review at your convenience. Did you purchase this book from kathleenjasper.com? If so, you can leave a review on Facebook, Google, or directly on our website on the product page. Thank you so much.

Check out my other products.

I have built several comprehensive, self-paced online courses for many teacher certification exams. I also have other books, webinars, and more. Go to https://kathleenjasper.com/ and use the offer code **5024** for 10% off any of my products.

If you have any questions, please contact us at info@kathleenjasper.com. It will be our pleasure to help. Good luck with your exam.

– Kathleen Jasper, Ed.D.

Follow me on social media. @kathleenjasperEdD @kathleen_jasper

 KathleenJasperEdD @kj_kathleenjasper @kathleenjasper

This page intentionally left blank.

Table of Contents

This page intentionally left blank.

About the Praxis Education of Young Children (5024) study guide

This study guide is aligned with the test specifications and blueprint of the Praxis Education of Young Children 5024 exam. All the sections of the study guide and content follow the organizational structure of the test specifications for the exam. We recommend downloading the ETS study companion for this test and reviewing its contents. You can do that by googling "Praxis 5024 study companion."

The following is the overall structure of the study guide:

1. Childhood Development and Learning
2. Observation, Documentation, and Assessment
3. Developmentally Appropriate Practices
4. Professionalism, Family, and Community
5. Content Pedagogy and Knowledge
6. Knowledge of Teaching – Constructed Response (CR)

After each content category is a mini practice test with ten test questions and detailed answer explanations. At the end of the study guide is a full-length practice test with 120 questions and detailed answer explanations.

Following the practice test there is comprehensive constructed response practice with sample answers for you to practice your writing.

Finally, the back of the study guide contains a **Good Words List** that details good words and phrases to look for in the correct answer choices on this exam.

You can learn more about our *good words* strategy and our *Think Like a Test Maker*™ methods by going to the Kathleen Jasper YouTube channel and watching the videos in our *Test Strategy* playlist.

Test Structure

The Education of Young Children test aligns with the National Association for the Education of Young Children (NAEYC) standards and the Common Core State Standards. It focuses on a teaching approach that encourages young children to actively engage in a variety of play and child-centered activities, providing opportunities for choice, decision-making, and discovery.

The test evaluates the examinee's knowledge of pedagogy, content, the application of theory to practice, and how theoretical concepts are implemented in educational settings. Additionally, it considers multicultural influences, diversity, developmental variations (including atypical development), and their impact on children's development and learning.

Test Structure and Content

Test Name	Praxis Education of Young Children (5024)
Time	2 hours 30 minutes
Number of Questions	120 selected-response 3 constructed-response
Test Format	The test consists of selected-response questions. You may have questions that ask you to choose all or some that apply. Other questions will have only one correct answer. The test is delivered on the computer and may contain some audio and visual elements. You may have additional questions on your exam that do not count toward your score.

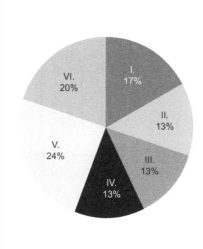

Content Category	Approx. Number of Questions	Approx. Percentage of Exam
I. Childhood Development and Learning	25	17%
II. Observation, Documentation, and Assessment	19	13%
III. Developmentally Appropriate Practices	19	13%
IV. Professionalism, Family, and Community	19	13%
V. Content Pedagogy and Knowledge	38	24%
VI. Knowledge of Teaching – Constructed Response (CR)	3	20%

I. Childhood Development and Learning

Understanding child development and learning is crucial for early childhood educators because it enables them to create developmentally appropriate learning experiences that cater to the diverse needs of young children. Knowledge of physical, cognitive, social, emotional, and language development helps educators design activities that support holistic growth, fostering a positive and stimulating environment where children can thrive. This understanding allows teachers to identify and address individual differences, provide targeted support, and use effective strategies to motivate and engage students, ultimately laying a strong foundation for lifelong learning and development.

The following concepts are discussed in this content category:

- Child Development
- Motivation
- Cultural and Linguistic Contexts for Development
- Developmentally Appropriate Practices
- Special Education
- Typical and Atypical Development
- Theory and Research

Child Development

Understanding the multiple interrelated areas of childhood development is crucial for providing comprehensive and effective instruction in early childhood education. The key areas in childhood development and learning include physical, cognitive, social, emotional, and language development.

1. Physical Development

Physical development in early childhood includes gross motor skills (large movements such as running, jumping, and climbing) and fine motor skills (small movements such as drawing, writing, and manipulating small objects).

- **Gross Motor Skills**: In the PreK-3 range, children develop their ability to control and coordinate their large muscles. Teachers can support this development through outdoor play, obstacle courses, and physical education classes.
- **Fine Motor Skills**: These skills are essential for tasks such as writing and cutting. Activities like coloring, using scissors, and playing with building blocks help refine these skills.

2. Cognitive Development

Cognitive development refers to how children think, explore, and figure things out. It includes skills such as problem-solving, memory, and decision-making.

- **Problem-Solving**: Teachers can encourage cognitive development by providing children with puzzles, problem-solving games, and opportunities for critical thinking.
- **Memory**: Activities that involve repetition and practice, such as songs and rhymes, help enhance memory skills.
- **Conceptual Understanding**: Introducing basic math and science concepts through hands-on activities and experiments fosters cognitive growth.

3. Social Development

Social development involves learning to interact with others, understanding social norms, and developing relationships.

- **Interaction with Peers**: Cooperative play, group projects, and classroom discussions help children learn to share, take turns, and communicate effectively.
- **Understanding Social Norms**: Teachers model and teach appropriate behaviors and social norms, such as respect, empathy, and cooperation.
- **Relationship Building**: Creating a positive classroom environment where children feel safe and valued supports the development of healthy relationships.

4. Emotional Development

Emotional development is about understanding and managing emotions, developing self-regulation, and building self-esteem.

- **Self-Regulation**: Teachers can help children learn to manage their emotions through activities that teach coping strategies, such as mindfulness exercises and calm-down techniques.
- **Self-Esteem**: Positive reinforcement, recognizing achievements, and fostering a growth mindset help build children's confidence and self-worth.
- **Understanding Emotions**: Activities that involve role-playing, storytelling, and discussing feelings can help children recognize and express their emotions appropriately.

5. Language Development

Language development encompasses both verbal and non-verbal communication skills.

- **Verbal Communication**: Teachers support language development by engaging children in conversations, reading aloud, and encouraging them to express their thoughts and ideas.
- **Non-Verbal Communication**: Understanding body language, facial expressions, and gestures is also important. Teachers can use visual aids and gestures to enhance communication.
- **Vocabulary and Grammar**: Introducing new vocabulary through stories, songs, and interactive activities helps expand children's language skills. Correcting grammar gently and modeling proper usage also supports language development.

Interconnections Among Developmental Areas

Each area of development is interconnected and influences the others. For example:

- **Language and Cognitive Development**: As children's language skills improve, so does their ability to understand and solve problems.
- **Physical and Social Development**: Participating in physical activities often involves social interactions, helping children develop motor and social skills.
- **Emotional and Cognitive Development**: Children who manage their emotions can better focus and engage in cognitive tasks.

Practical Strategies for Teachers

- **Integrated Learning Activities**: Plan activities that address multiple developmental areas simultaneously, such as a group project that involves building (physical), planning (cognitive), discussing (language), and collaborating (social).
- **Individualized Instruction**: Recognize that each child develops independently and tailor instruction to meet diverse needs.
- **Positive Classroom Environment**: Create a supportive and nurturing environment that encourages exploration and learning across all developmental areas.

By understanding and supporting these interconnected areas of development, PreK-3 teachers can provide a holistic education that fosters their students' overall growth and well-being.

Motivation

Understanding the factors that affect children's motivation is essential for creating an engaging and supportive learning environment. Multiple factors influence children's motivation. Teachers can use this information to design activities and practices that motivate young children in the classroom and on the playground.

Intrinsic motivation refers to engaging in a behavior because it is inherently interesting or enjoyable. When children are intrinsically motivated, they participate in an activity for the sake of the activity and the personal satisfaction it brings rather than for some separable consequence or external reward.

- **Characteristics of Intrinsic Motivation**:
  - **Curiosity and Interest**: Children are naturally curious and are motivated to learn about topics that interest them.
  - **Sense of Competence**: Children who feel capable and successful are motivated to continue engaging in activities.
  - **Autonomy**: Allowing children to make choices and have some control over their activities can boost their intrinsic motivation.
- **Examples of Intrinsic Motivation**:
  - A child reads a book because they find the story fascinating.
  - A student solves a puzzle because they enjoy the challenge.
  - An individual plays a musical instrument because they love music.

Extrinsic motivation involves engaging in a behavior to earn external rewards or to avoid negative consequences. The motivation comes from outside the individual, such as praise, grades, money, or the approval of others.

- **Characteristics of Extrinsic Motivation**:
  - **External Rewards**: The behavior is driven by anticipating external rewards.
  - **Avoidance of Punishment**: The behavior is performed to avoid negative outcomes or disapproval.
  - **Compliance with Expectations**: The individual may engage in the activity to meet external expectations or requirements.
- **Examples of Extrinsic Motivation**:
  - Students study to earn good grades or to avoid failing.
  - A child cleans up after an activity to receive a star on the clean-up chart.
  - Students complete their classroom assignments to avoid extra homework.

Other motivational factors include:

- **Social Factors**
  - **Peer Interactions**: Positive social interactions and collaborative activities can enhance motivation.
  - **Teacher Relationships**: A supportive and caring relationship with teachers can significantly impact a child's motivation.
- **Environmental Factors**
  - **Classroom and Playground Environment**: A stimulating and engaging environment can inspire motivation. Safe, well-organized, and resource-rich spaces are more likely to motivate children.
  - **Access to Resources**: Access to various learning materials and playground equipment can keep children engaged and motivated.

- **Personal Factors**
  - **Individual Interests**: Children are more motivated when activities align with their personal interests and preferences.
  - **Self-Efficacy**: Children's belief in their ability to succeed influences their motivation to engage in tasks.

Five Strategies for Motivating Young Children

Teachers can use the following strategies to use their knowledge of student motivation to inspire students to meet their potential and to persevere in their learning.

1. **Foster a Love for Learning**
   - **Incorporate Interests**: Integrate topics that interest the children into the curriculum. For example, if a child loves dinosaurs, include dinosaur-related books and activities.
   - **Hands-On Activities**: Use interactive and hands-on activities to make learning fun and engaging.

2. **Build a Supportive Environment**
   - **Positive Reinforcement**: Use praise and encouragement to acknowledge children's efforts and achievements.
   - **Classroom Community**: Create a sense of community where children feel safe, respected, and valued.

3. **Promote Autonomy**
   - **Choice and Control**: Offer choices in activities and allow children to take the lead in some tasks, fostering a sense of independence and control.

4. **Set Realistic and Achievable Goals**
   - **Incremental Challenges**: Provide tasks that are challenging yet achievable to help children experience success and build confidence.

5. **Use Varied Teaching Methods**
   - **Differentiated Instruction**: Tailor activities to meet the diverse needs and learning styles of the children.
   - **Interactive Lessons**: Incorporate technology, storytelling, music, and movement to keep children engaged.

On the Playground

Early childhood students spend lots of time on the playground. Therefore, teachers must understand how to apply the concepts of child development and motivation to encourage students' interactive play.

1. **Encourage Physical Activity**
   - **Variety of Equipment**: Provide a range of playground equipment that caters to different interests and skill levels, such as swings, slides, climbing structures, and sports equipment.
   - **Organized Games**: Organize group games and activities that promote teamwork and physical exercise.

2. **Promote Social Interaction**
   - **Group Play**: Encourage cooperative play and group activities to help children develop social skills and friendships.
   - **Conflict Resolution**: Teach children how to resolve conflicts and work together, fostering a positive social environment.

3. **Ensure a Safe and Inclusive Environment**

- **Safety Measures**: Ensure the playground is safe and children feel secure while playing.

- **Inclusivity**: Create an inclusive environment where all children can participate and enjoy the activities regardless of their abilities.

4. **Incorporate Learning Opportunities**

- **Educational Play**: Integrate educational elements into play, such as nature walks, scavenger hunts, and exploration activities, to encourage curiosity and learning.

5. **Recognize and Celebrate Achievements**

- **Positive Feedback**: Provide positive feedback and celebrate big and small achievements to encourage continued effort and participation.

By understanding these factors and implementing these strategies, teachers can effectively motivate young children, making both the classroom and the playground engaging and nurturing environments for learning and growth.

Classroom Scenario: First-Grade Science

The following outlines a first-grade class in which the teacher leverages her knowledge of child development and motivation to create an engaging and effective learning environment.

Learning Objective: Students will be able to identify and describe the parts of a plant (roots, stem, leaves, flowers) and explain their functions, demonstrating their understanding through a hands-on planting activity and a group-created chart.

Setting the Stage

The classroom is brightly decorated with posters of different plants and a designated learning corner with potted plants, gardening tools, and picture books about plants. The teacher, Ms. Johnson, has set up a small table with various seeds, soil, and pots for a hands-on planting activity.

Introduction (10 minutes)

Ms. Johnson gathers the students on the rug for circle time. She begins with a story about a sunflower named Sunny, who grows tall and strong by getting everything it needs from its environment.

- **Intrinsic Motivation**: The story captivates the students' interest and curiosity about plants.

- **Cognitive Development**: The story provides a narrative framework for understanding plant growth.

Interactive Discussion (10 minutes)

After the story, Ms. Johnson shows real plants and uses visual aids to explain the different parts of a plant (roots, stem, leaves, flowers). She encourages the students to ask questions and share their experiences with plants.

- **Language Development**: The discussion helps students practice their vocabulary and speaking skills.

- **Social Development**: The interactive format promotes communication and turn-taking.

Hands-On Activity (20 minutes)

Ms. Johnson then moves to the planting activity. Each student gets to plant their seed in a small pot. She explains the steps and guides them through the process, encouraging them to get their hands dirty and explore the soil and seeds.

- **Physical Development**: The activity involves fine motor skills as students handle seeds and soil.

- **Intrinsic Motivation**: The hands-on nature of the activity makes it enjoyable and engaging.

Group Project (15 minutes)

Ms. Johnson organizes the students into small groups. Each group is given a chart with different plant parts and is asked to draw and label them. They also discuss what plants need to grow (water, sunlight, soil).

- **Social Development**: Working in groups fosters collaboration and teamwork.
- **Cognitive Development**: Creating charts helps reinforce the students' understanding of plant parts and their functions.

Reflection and Sharing (10 minutes)

Ms. Johnson invites each group to share their charts in the circle and explain what they learned. She praises their efforts and gives each student a sticker for their participation.

- **Extrinsic Motivation**: The stickers serve as a reward, reinforcing positive behavior and effort.
- **Emotional Development**: Sharing their work helps build confidence and self-esteem.

Conclusion and Wrap-Up (5 minutes)

Ms. Johnson wraps up the lesson by summarizing the key points and reading a short poem about plants. She encourages the students to observe their plants at home and think about what they need to grow.

- **Intrinsic Motivation**: The poem provides a pleasant and engaging conclusion to the lesson.
- **Cognitive Development**: The summary reinforces the day's learning objectives.

Key Elements in the Scenario

- **Integrated Learning**: The lesson incorporates storytelling, hands-on activities, group work, and reflection, addressing multiple developmental areas.
- **Motivation Strategies**: Ms. Johnson uses intrinsic (interesting story, hands-on activity) and extrinsic (stickers) motivation techniques.
- **Supportive Environment**: The classroom is designed to be visually stimulating and resource-rich, providing a conducive environment for learning.
- **Positive Reinforcement**: Praise and rewards are used to recognize and encourage student participation and effort.

By applying her knowledge of child development and motivation, Ms. Johnson creates a dynamic and supportive learning experience that maximizes student engagement and fosters holistic growth.

Cultural and Linguistic Contexts for Development

Early childhood educators must recognize and understand the various factors impacting a child's development and learning. This awareness allows teachers to create supportive and inclusive environments tailored to each child's needs.

Diverse Cultural and Linguistic Contexts for Development

Children come from various cultural backgrounds and may speak different languages at home. These cultural and linguistic contexts shape their experiences, values, and ways of learning.

- **Application**:
  - **Cultural Sensitivity**: Integrate culturally relevant materials and activities into the curriculum to reflect and respect the diversity of the classroom.
  - **Language Support**: Support children who are English Language Learners (ELLs) by providing resources, such as bilingual books and visual aids.
  - **Inclusive Environment**: Celebrate cultural differences through multicultural events and encourage the sharing of cultural practices to foster mutual respect and understanding.

Health Status and Disabilities

A child's physical health, including disabilities or chronic conditions, can significantly impact their learning and development.

- **Application**:
  - **Health Awareness**: Stay informed about each child's health needs and collaborate with families and healthcare professionals to accommodate these needs in the classroom.
  - **Inclusive Practices**: Implement strategies such as differentiated instruction and Universal Design for Learning (UDL) to ensure all children, including those with disabilities, can access and participate in the curriculum.
  - **Support Services**: To assist children with specific needs, utilize support services such as special education resources, occupational therapy, and speech therapy.

Family and Community Characteristics

The characteristics of a child's family and community, including socioeconomic status, family structure, and community resources, play a crucial role in their development and learning.

- **Application**:
  - **Family Engagement**: Build strong partnerships with families by maintaining open communication, involving them in classroom activities, and respecting their insights and contributions.
  - **Community Resources**: Leverage community resources such as libraries, cultural centers, and local organizations to enrich the educational experience and support children and families.
  - **Socioeconomic Awareness**: Be sensitive to families' socioeconomic challenges and provide equitable access to learning opportunities and materials for all children.

How Teachers Can Use This Knowledge to Be Better Early Childhood Educators

1. **Holistic Approach**: Adopt a holistic approach to teaching that considers the whole child, addressing not just cognitive development but also social, emotional, physical, and language needs.
2. **Personalized Learning**: Tailor instruction to meet the diverse needs of each child by understanding their backgrounds, health conditions, and family dynamics.
3. **Creating Inclusive Classrooms**: Develop inclusive classroom environments where all children feel valued and supported, regardless of their cultural background, health status, or family circumstances.
4. **Effective Communication**: Foster strong communication with families and communities to build trust, gather valuable insights, and collaborate effectively to support each child's development.
5. **Professional Development**: Continuously seek professional development opportunities to stay informed about best practices and new research in child development, inclusive education, and cultural competence.
6. **Resource Utilization**: Use available resources and support systems, including special education services, community programs, and health professionals, to provide comprehensive support for all students.

Developmentally Appropriate Practices

Developmentally Appropriate Practices (DAP) in early childhood education refer to teaching methods and educational strategies that are based on the developmental stages and individual needs of young children. These practices are designed to promote optimal learning and development by considering what is known about child development, each child's strengths and needs, and the social and cultural contexts in which children live.

Key Components of Developmentally Appropriate Practices

Age Appropriateness: Educators must be aware of the typical developmental milestones and characteristics of different age groups. For example, toddlers explore their environment through sensory and motor activities, while preschoolers engage in more complex imaginative play.

Activities and experiences should match the developmental abilities of the age group, providing appropriate challenges that promote growth without causing frustration.

Individual Appropriateness: Each child is unique, with their own strengths, interests, and learning styles. Educators should observe and understand each child's individual development and adapt their teaching accordingly.

Providing differentiated instruction and a variety of learning experiences to meet the needs of each child, ensuring that all children can engage and learn effectively.

Cultural and Social Responsiveness: Children's backgrounds, including their cultural, linguistic, and familial contexts, significantly influence their learning and development. Educators should respect and incorporate these diverse backgrounds into the learning environment.

Building strong relationships with families and the community to support children's learning and development and to create a cohesive and inclusive educational experience.

Principles of Developmentally Appropriate Practices

1. **Creating a Caring Community of Learners**:
   - Foster a supportive, respectful, and inclusive classroom environment where children feel valued and connected.
   - Encourage positive relationships among children, families, and educators.

2. **Teaching to Enhance Development and Learning**:
   - Use a variety of teaching strategies and interactions that promote children's development and learning.
   - Implement intentional, purposeful teaching that is responsive to children's needs and interests.

3. **Planning Curriculum to Achieve Important Goals**:
   - Develop a well-planned, coherent curriculum that addresses all areas of development: cognitive, social, emotional, physical, and linguistic.
   - Ensure that learning experiences are meaningful, engaging, and aligned with developmental goals.

4. **Assessing Children's Development and Learning**:
   - Use ongoing, formative assessment to understand and support each child's learning and development.
   - Collect information through observations, work samples, and discussions to inform instructional decisions and communicate progress with families.

5. **Establishing Reciprocal Relationships with Families**:
   - Build strong, respectful partnerships with families, recognizing them as integral to their child's education.
   - Communicate regularly with families about their child's development and involve them in the educational process.

Implementation of Developmentally Appropriate Practices

- **Play-Based Learning**: Incorporate play as a central component of the curriculum, recognizing that play is a vital way children learn and develop.

- **Hands-On Activities**: Use manipulatives, sensory experiences, and interactive activities that engage children actively in their learning process.

- **Flexible Classroom Environment**: Arrange the classroom to allow for various types of activities, such as individual work, small group collaboration, and large group instruction, adapting to children's changing needs.

- **Positive Guidance**: Use positive behavior management techniques that promote self-regulation and social competence, avoiding punitive measures.

- **Integrated Learning**: Create interdisciplinary lessons that connect different areas of learning, helping children make meaningful connections across subjects.

Typical and Atypical Development

Being familiar with the range of typical and atypical development is essential for early childhood educators to provide high-quality, individualized, and inclusive education. This knowledge enables educators to identify and support the unique needs of each child, tailor instruction to promote optimal development, create inclusive and supportive learning environments, collaborate effectively with families and specialists, and implement timely interventions. Ultimately, this comprehensive understanding ensures that all children, regardless of their developmental trajectory, can succeed and reach their full potential.

The previous chart is certainly not an exhaustive list. However, when teachers are aware of typical and atypical development, they can better understand and help their students.

Age	Physical Development	Cognitive Development	Social Development	Emotional Development	Linguistic Development
Birth to 1 year	Gains control over head, arms, and legs. Begins to roll over, sit, crawl, and stand with support	Explores environment through senses. Recognizes familiar faces. Develops object permanence.	Begins to form attachments to caregivers. Smiles and responds to social stimuli	Expresses basic emotions (e.g., joy, distress.) Develops attachment and trust.	Babbles and coos. Responds to name. Begins to say simple words like "mama" and "dada."
1 to 2 years	Walks independently. Begins to run. Stacks blocks. Uses utensils.	Engages in simple problem-solving. Begins to understand cause and effect. Imitates actions.	Starts parallel play (playing alongside others without interaction). Shows preference for certain people	Shows more complex emotions (e.g., jealousy, pride). Begins to develop self-awareness	Vocabulary rapidly expands. Uses two-word phrases. Follows simple instructions

Age	Physical Development	Cognitive Development	Social Development	Emotional Development	Linguistic Development
2 to 3 years	Climbs on furniture. Kicks and throws a ball. Begins potty training.	Engages in pretend play. Understands simple concepts (big/little, up/down). Begins to sort objects by shape and color.	Begins associative play (interacting with others in play activities). Develops basic friendships.	Demonstrates increased independence. Begins to cope with emotions, though tantrums are common.	Uses three to four-word sentences. Understands and uses pronouns. Asks questions.
3 to 4 years	Hops and stands on one foot. Pedals a tricycle. Draws basic shapes	Begins to understand time (yesterday, today, tomorrow). Solves simple puzzles. Recognizes some letters and numbers	Engages in cooperative play. Takes turns and shares with others. Shows concern for peers	Expresses a wider range of emotions. Begins to understand the concept of right and wrong	Uses complex sentences. Knows basic grammar rules. Tells simple stories
4 to 5 years	Catches and throws a ball more accurately. Dresses and undresses without help. Uses scissors.	Understands counting and basic math concepts. Recognizes and writes some letters and numbers. Engages in more complex pretend play.	Understands and follows rules. Plays group games. Develops deeper friendships.	Better manages emotions Shows empathy and caring for others.	Uses future tense. Understands more complex grammar. Tells more detailed stories.
5 to 6 years	Skips and hops on one foot. Rides a bicycle with training wheels. Draws more detailed pictures	Begins to read simple words. Understands basic addition and subtraction. Thinks more logically and concretely.	Participates in group activities and structured games. Understands others' perspectives better.	Shows more self-control and coping strategies. Begins to develop a self-concept	Speaks in full sentences. Uses a more extensive vocabulary. Begins to write simple sentences
6 to 8 years	Develops better coordination and balance. Rides a bicycle without training wheels. Engages in team sports	Reads fluently with comprehension. Solves more complex math problems. Understands more abstract concepts	Forms stronger peer relationships. Works well in groups. Develops a sense of belonging to a group.	Demonstrates increased independence. Manages a wider range of emotions. Develops a clearer sense of self-esteem	Writes more complex sentences and stories. Understands and uses figurative language. Communicates effectively in conversations

Identifying Individual Needs

- **Gifted and Talented**: Recognizing gifted and talented children enables educators to provide advanced and enriched learning opportunities that challenge and stimulate their intellectual curiosity, preventing boredom and disengagement.

- **Learning Delays**: Early identification of learning delays allows educators to implement timely interventions and support strategies, helping children overcome challenges and catch up with their peers.

- **Dual-Language Learners**: Understanding the unique needs of dual-language learners helps educators create a supportive environment that fosters language development in their native language and English, promoting bilingualism and cognitive flexibility.

- **Developmental Disabilities**: Being aware of developmental disabilities ensures that educators can adapt their teaching methods and classroom environment to accommodate the specific needs of these children, providing inclusive education that supports their growth and learning.

Tailoring Instruction

- **Differentiated Instruction**: Knowledge of typical and atypical development allows educators to differentiate instruction, providing varied learning experiences that cater to the classroom's diverse abilities and learning styles.

- **Scaffolded Learning**: Educators can use scaffolding techniques to provide appropriate levels of support based on each child's developmental stage, gradually reducing assistance as the child becomes more capable and confident.

Quick Tip

Universal Design for Learning (UDL) is an educational framework that aims to create a flexible learning environment that accommodates all students' diverse needs. By proactively designing curricula that include multiple means of representation, expression, and engagement, UDL ensures that learning materials and activities are accessible and challenging for students with varying abilities, learning styles, and backgrounds. This approach promotes inclusivity and equity in education by removing barriers and providing all students with equal opportunities to succeed.

Creating Inclusive Environments

- **Inclusive Practices**: Familiarity with atypical development ensures that educators can implement inclusive practices that make all children feel valued and accepted, fostering a positive and supportive classroom climate.

- **Universal Design for Learning (UDL)**: Educators can apply UDL principles to design learning experiences that are accessible and beneficial for all children, regardless of their developmental differences.

Collaborating with Families and Specialists

- **Family Engagement**: Understanding the range of developmental trajectories allows educators to communicate effectively with families, providing valuable insights and involving them in their child's learning process.

- **Interdisciplinary Collaboration**: Educators can work collaboratively with specialists, such as speech therapists, occupational therapists, and special education professionals, to provide comprehensive support tailored to each child's needs.

Early Intervention and Support

- **Timely Interventions**: Early recognition of atypical development allows for timely interventions, which is crucial for addressing developmental issues before they become more pronounced and challenging to remediate.

- **Support Services**: Educators can connect children and families with appropriate support services and resources, ensuring they receive the help they need to thrive.

Quick Tip

Remember, cognitive ability is shaped by both genetic factors and environmental influences. A stimulating and supportive learning environment can significantly enhance a child's cognitive development. When considering assessment questions, consider how the classroom environment, family background, and access to resources play critical roles in shaping a child's learning and growth.

Special Education

Special education in early childhood education focuses on providing individualized support and interventions to young children with diverse learning needs, disabilities, or developmental delays from birth to age eight. This approach emphasizes early identification and assessment to tailor educational plans that foster the child's cognitive, social, emotional, and physical development.

Special education services often include speech therapy, occupational therapy, physical therapy, and specialized instructional strategies to create an inclusive environment where all children can thrive. Collaboration among educators, families, and specialists is key to ensuring that each child receives the necessary resources and support to reach their full potential.

What is an IEP?

An Individualized Education Program (IEP) is a critical document for children with disabilities and is a cornerstone of special education services in the United States. Mandated by the Individuals with Disabilities Education Act (IDEA), the IEP is both a process and a product that ensures a child with a recognized disability receives personalized instruction and services tailored to their unique learning needs.

The IEP is developed by a team that typically includes:

- The child's parents or guardians

- At least one of the child's general education teachers (if applicable)

- At least one special education teacher or provider

- A representative of the school system who is knowledgeable about the general curriculum and the availability of resources

- An individual who can interpret the instructional implications of evaluation results (this can be a team member already mentioned)

- Others at the discretion of the parents or school

- The child, when appropriate, especially when transition services are being discussed

Quick Tip

By law, the Individualized Education Program (IEP) is reviewed and revised annually by the IEP team to assess progress and update goals, accommodations, and services based on the child's evolving needs. This collaborative process ensures that the educational plan remains relevant and effective in supporting the child's development. Input from teachers, parents, and specialists is integral to tailoring the IEP to address the child's unique strengths and challenges.

The IEP outlines the following:

1. **Current Performance**: A detailed description of the child's current academic and functional performance, which includes how the child's disability affects their involvement and progress in the general education curriculum.

2. **Annual Goals**: Specific, measurable educational goals for the child to achieve in the academic year, which are designed to meet their needs that result from the disability and to enable them to make progress in the general education curriculum.

3. **Special Education and Related Services**: The specific special education and related services that will be provided to the child, including supplementary aids and services, modifications, or accommodations provided in the classroom or other settings.

4. **Participation with Non-Disabled Children**: An explanation of the extent to which the child will not participate with non-disabled children in the regular class and other school activities.

5. **Participation in State and District-Wide Assessments**: The accommodations necessary for the child to participate in state or district-wide assessments or the justification for why a separate assessment is needed.

6. **Dates and Places**: When services and modifications will begin, how often they will be provided, where they will be provided, and their duration.

7. **Transition Services**: For students who will reach the age of transition during the IEP period, a plan for transition services to post-school activities, including post-secondary education, vocational education, integrated employment, continuing and adult education, adult services, independent living, or community participation.

8. **Progress Measurement**: How the child's progress toward meeting the annual goals will be measured and how the child's parents will be informed of that progress.

The IEP is a legally binding document, and schools are required to implement all its components as written. The IEP is developed in an IEP meeting and must be reviewed at least annually to determine whether the annual goals are being achieved and to revise the IEP as appropriate to address any lack of expected progress.

What is IDEA?

The Individuals with Disabilities Education Act (IDEA) is a federal law in the United States that mandates the provision of free and appropriate public education (FAPE) to children with disabilities. IDEA ensures that children with disabilities have the same opportunities for education as those children who do not have disabilities.

Key components of IDEA include:

1. **Individualized Education Program (IEP)**: IDEA requires the creation of an IEP for each child with a disability, which is tailored to their individual needs and outlines specific educational goals, services, and accommodations.

2. **Free and Appropriate Public Education (FAPE)**: Schools must provide students with disabilities a free education that is tailored to their individual needs as outlined in their IEP at no cost to the family.

3. **Least Restrictive Environment (LRE)**: IDEA stipulates that children with disabilities should be educated to the greatest extent appropriate with peers who do not have disabilities. This principle promotes inclusion and access to general education classrooms and curricula.

4. **Appropriate Evaluation**: Before providing special education, schools must conduct comprehensive evaluations to determine if a child has a disability and what their educational needs are.

5. **Parent and Teacher Participation**: IDEA ensures that parents and teachers are involved in the decision-making process regarding the child's education. This includes participation in the development of the IEP and decisions about placement.

6. **Procedural Safeguards**: The law provides a set of procedural safeguards designed to protect the rights of children with disabilities and their families. This includes the right to confidentiality, the right to review educational records, and the right to dispute resolutions such as mediation and due process hearings.

7. **Early Intervention**: IDEA Part C covers early intervention services for infants and toddlers with disabilities, which includes services from birth through age two. This is followed by transition to preschool services.

IDEA is central to special education in the U.S. and has undergone several updates since its initial passage in 1975 (originally named the Education for All Handicapped Children Act). These updates have continued to refine and expand the scope of services and protections to ensure an inclusive and equitable education for all children with disabilities.

Theory and Research

To do well on the exam, you must know the major early childhood education theorists. The following are some of the main early childhood education theorists and their contributions to the education of young children:

Jean Piaget proposed a theory of cognitive development that outlines how children's thinking evolves through four stages: sensorimotor, preoperational, concrete operational, and formal operational. Piaget's work emphasized the importance of active learning and discovery, highlighting that children construct knowledge through hands-on experiences and interactions with their environment. His theories have significantly influenced educational practices, promoting student-centered, experiential learning approaches in classrooms.

- **Contribution**: Piaget's theory of cognitive development outlines how children's thinking evolves through four stages: sensorimotor, preoperational, concrete operational, and formal operational.

- **Impact on Education**: His work emphasizes the importance of hands-on learning and discovery, suggesting that children learn best through play and active exploration of their environment.

Piaget's Stages of Cognitive Development

Stage	Age Range	Characteristics	Key Developmental Milestones
Sensorimotor	Birth to 2 years	Learning through sensory experiences and manipulating objects	Object permanence: Understanding that objects continue to exist even when they cannot be seen, heard, or touched. Beginning of goal-directed actions
Preoperational	2 to 7 years	Development of language and symbolic thinking. Egocentrism: Difficulty seeing things from perspectives other than their own.	Symbolic play: Using objects or symbols to represent other things (e.g., pretend play) Animism: Belief that inanimate objects have lifelike qualities. Rapid language development.

Stage	Age Range	Characteristics	Key Developmental Milestones
Concrete Operational	7 to 11 years	Logical thinking about concrete events. Understanding of conservation and perspective-taking.	Conservation: Understanding that quantity remains the same despite changes in shape or appearance. Classification: Ability to group objects based on common characteristics.
Formal Operational	11 years and up	Abstract and hypothetical thinking. Systematic planning and problem-solving.	Abstract reasoning: Thinking about concepts that are not physically present. Hypothetical-deductive reasoning: Ability to formulate and test hypotheses in a logical manner.

Lev Vygotsky introduced the concept of the Zone of Proximal Development (ZPD) and emphasized the role of social interaction and cultural context in learning. His theories highlight the importance of scaffolding and guided learning, where teachers and peers support children in reaching higher levels of understanding and skill.

Gradual Release of Responsibility Model (GRR)

The Gradual Release of Responsibility (GRR) model typically includes four stages:

1. **I Do (Direct Instruction)**: The teacher models the task, providing clear examples and explanations.

2. **We Do (Guided Practice)**: The teacher and students work together on the task, with the teacher providing support and scaffolding.

3. **You Do Together (Collaborative Practice)**: Students work in pairs or small groups to complete the task, helping each other while the teacher monitors and offers assistance as needed.

4. **You Do (Independent Practice)**: Students work independently on the task, applying what they have learned with minimal teacher assistance.

Quick Tip

The gradual release of responsibility method is an example of applying the Zone of Proximal Development (ZPD) in the classroom. The ZPD concept refers to the difference between what a learner can do independently and what they can achieve with guidance and support. Gradual release aligns with this by providing a structured approach to teaching that moves from teacher-directed instruction to independent student work, effectively supporting students within their ZPD.

Example Scenario

In Mr. Jones's second-grade classroom, he uses the gradual release method to teach story sequencing. First, he reads a story aloud and models how to identify the beginning, middle, and end (I Do). Next, he reads another story with the class, asking students to help him sequence the events (We Do). Then, students pair up to sequence a short story using picture cards, discussing their choices with each other (You Do Together). Finally, each student independently sequences a new story, demonstrating their understanding (You Do). Throughout the process, Mr. Jones provides support as needed, gradually releasing responsibility as students become more confident and capable, effectively working within their ZPD.

Erik Erikson is credited with the psychosocial theory of development, which describes eight stages of human development, each characterized by a different psychological conflict. In early childhood, the stages of trust vs. mistrust, autonomy vs. shame and doubt, and initiative vs. guilt emphasize the importance of fostering a secure, supportive environment that promotes independence and initiative.

The following are the eight stages of human development according to Erik Erikson, along with the central psychosocial conflict associated with each stage:

1. **Trust vs. Mistrust**

   - Infancy (birth to 18 months)

   - Developing trust when caregivers provide reliability, care, and affection. A lack of this leads to mistrust.

2. **Autonomy vs. Shame and Doubt**

   - Early Childhood (18 months to 3 years)

   - Developing a sense of personal control over physical skills and a sense of independence. Success leads to feelings of autonomy, while failure results in feelings of shame and doubt.

3. **Initiative vs. Guilt**

   - Preschool (3 to 5 years)

   - Beginning to assert control and power over the environment. Success in this stage leads to a sense of initiative, while failure results in feelings of guilt.

4. **Industry vs. Inferiority**

   - School Age (5 to 12 years)

   - Coping with new social and academic demands. Success leads to a sense of competence, while failure results in feelings of inferiority.

5. **Identity vs. Role Confusion**

   - Adolescence (12 to 18 years)

   - Developing a sense of self and personal identity. Success leads to an ability to stay true to oneself, while failure leads to role confusion and a weak sense of self.

6. **Intimacy vs. Isolation**

   - Young Adulthood (18 to 40 years)

   - Forming intimate, loving relationships with other people. Success leads to strong relationships, while failure results in loneliness and isolation.

7. **Generativity vs. Stagnation**

   - Middle Adulthood (40 to 65 years)

   - Creating or nurturing things that will outlast oneself, often by parenting children or contributing to positive changes that benefit others. Success leads to feelings of usefulness and accomplishment, while failure results in shallow involvement in the world.

8. **Integrity vs. Despair**

   - Late Adulthood (65 years and older)

   - Reflecting on one's life and feeling a sense of fulfillment. Success at this stage leads to feelings of wisdom, while failure results in regret, bitterness, and despair.

Maria Montessori developed the Montessori Method based on self-directed activity, hands-on learning, and collaborative play. Her approach encourages independence, freedom within limits, and respect for a child's natural psychological development.

Main Characteristics of Montessori Schools

1. **Child-Centered Learning**: Learning is tailored to each child's individual needs, interests, and developmental pace. Children can choose their activities and work independently within a structured environment.

2. **Prepared Environment**: The classroom is meticulously arranged with child-sized furniture and accessible materials. The materials are designed to be aesthetically pleasing and to encourage exploration and learning. The environment is orderly and promotes independence.

3. **Hands-On Learning**: Montessori materials emphasize tactile and sensory experiences. Learning is achieved through hands-on activities that engage multiple senses, promoting deeper understanding.

4. **Mixed-Age Classrooms**: Classrooms typically have a three-year age range, allowing for peer learning and mentoring. Older children help younger ones, fostering a sense of community and collaboration.

5. **Focus on Independence**: Activities are designed to promote self-sufficiency and independence. Children are encouraged to care for their needs, such as preparing snacks, cleaning up, and managing personal belongings.

6. **Respect for the Child**: Teachers respect each child's individuality and developmental pace. They value children's choices and voices and nurture their intrinsic motivation.

7. **Role of the Teacher**: Teachers act as guides or facilitators rather than traditional instructors. They observe and support the child's learning process, providing guidance and resources as needed. The teacher prepares the environment and introduces materials but allows children to learn through their own discovery.

8. **Integrated Curriculum**: Subjects are not taught in isolation; learning is interdisciplinary and integrated. Topics such as math, language, science, and cultural studies are interconnected, providing a holistic approach to education.

9. **Emphasis on Practical Life Skills**: Practical life activities are an essential part of the curriculum, teaching children everyday skills such as pouring, sweeping, dressing, and gardening. These activities develop fine motor skills, concentration, and a sense of responsibility.

10. **Intrinsic Motivation**: Learning activities are designed to be intrinsically rewarding, encouraging children to learn for the joy of discovery rather than for external rewards.

11. **Sensorial Education**: Materials and activities are designed to refine the five senses and help children understand and classify their sensory experiences.

12. **Peace Education and Social Responsibility**: Montessori education promotes peace, respect, and social responsibility. Children are taught conflict resolution, empathy, and global awareness.

13. **Self-Correction and Assessment**: Materials are designed to allow for self-correction, enabling children to learn from their mistakes. Assessment is ongoing and based on observation rather than standardized tests.

Abraham Maslow established a hierarchy of needs, outlining human needs from basic physiological needs to self-actualization. His theory underscores the importance of meeting children's basic needs to provide a stable foundation for learning and development.

This hierarchy outlines sequential fulfillment, meaning the most basic physiological needs for survival (e.g., food, water, shelter). Once these are met, individuals can focus on safety needs (e.g., security, stability). Once those are met, individuals can focus on Love and belonging needs.

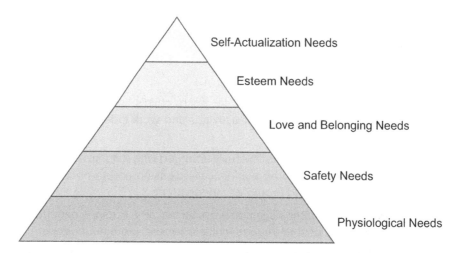

1. **Physiological Needs:**

   - Definition: These are the basic biological requirements for human survival.

   - Examples: Air, water, food, shelter, sleep, clothing, and reproduction.

   - Importance: These needs are the most fundamental and must be met first. The human body cannot function properly if these needs are not satisfied.

2. **Safety Needs:**

   - Definition: Once physiological needs are met, the need for safety and security becomes prominent.

   - Examples: Personal security, financial security, health and well-being, safety against accidents and injury.

   - Importance: These needs are crucial for stability and protection from physical and emotional harm.

3. **Love and Belonging Needs:**

   - Definition: These needs emerge after physiological and safety needs are fulfilled and emotional relationships are involved.

   - Examples: Friendship, intimacy, family, social groups, community, and sense of connection.

   - Importance: Meeting these needs helps individuals overcome feelings of loneliness and isolation and promotes social connections and acceptance.

4. **Esteem Needs:**

   - Definition: After the need for love and belonging is satisfied, esteem needs become important.

   - Examples: Self-esteem, respect from others, status, recognition, strength, freedom, and accomplishment.

   - Importance: Satisfying these needs leads to feelings of self-worth, confidence, and achievement. Unmet esteem needs can result in feelings of inferiority and helplessness.

5. **Self-Actualization Needs:**

   - Definition: This is the highest level of Maslow's hierarchy and involves realizing and fulfilling one's potential.

   - Examples: Pursuing personal growth, peak experiences, creativity, problem-solving, authenticity, and achieving personal goals.

   - Importance: Self-actualization is about becoming the best version of oneself. It represents the desire to accomplish everything that one can.

Quick Tip

Maslow's hierarchy of needs is a motivational focus. As each level of needs is met, an individual's motivational focus shifts upward to the next level. This hierarchical structure reflects a natural progression in human motivation.

The hierarchy suggests a pathway to holistic human development, where meeting each level of needs leads to greater well-being and personal growth.

John Dewey promoted progressive education, emphasizing the need for education to be rooted in real-life experiences and active learning. His ideas support experiential learning, critical thinking, and the development of problem-solving skills through interactive and practical experiences.

John Dewey's "learning by doing" concept is a fundamental principle of his educational philosophy, emphasizing the importance of active, experiential learning—learning should involve hands-on activities, real-world problem-solving, and practical applications of knowledge. Dewey believed that students learn best through direct experience and active participation rather than passive absorption of information.

Key Principles:

1. **Experiential Education**: Learning activities should be rooted in real-life experiences and practical tasks.

   Students engage in projects, experiments, and activities that require them to meaningfully apply what they are learning.

2. **Reflective Thinking**: After engaging in an activity, students should reflect on their experiences to deepen their understanding.

   Reflection helps students connect their actions and the underlying concepts or principles.

3. **Collaborative Learning**: Learning by doing often involves working in groups and promoting social interaction and cooperation.

   Students learn from each other's perspectives and develop important social and communication skills.

4. **Integrated Curriculum**: Dewey advocated for a curriculum integrating various subjects around central themes or projects.

   This approach helps students see the interconnectedness of knowledge and apply their learning comprehensively.

Dewey's "learning by doing" concept has had a lasting influence on progressive education, emphasizing that education should prepare students for active participation in a democratic society by developing their critical thinking, problem-solving, and collaborative skills through practical experiences.

Quick Tip

Constructivism is a learning theory that posits that individuals construct their own understanding and knowledge of the world through experiences and reflecting on those experiences. It emphasizes active engagement, hands-on activities, and learning through discovery and inquiry.

Howard Gardner proposed the theory of multiple intelligences, suggesting various types of intelligence, including linguistic, logical-mathematical, spatial, musical, bodily-kinesthetic, interpersonal, intrapersonal, and naturalistic. His theory encourages educators to recognize and nurture the different strengths and talents of each child, using diverse teaching strategies to reach all learners.

Type of Intelligence	Description	Examples of Activities	Strengths
Linguistic	Ability to use language effectively for communication and expression.	Reading, writing, storytelling, debating, learning languages.	Good at writing, speaking, and understanding complex verbal concepts.
Logical-Mathematical	Ability to think logically, reason, and solve mathematical problems.	Solving puzzles, conducting experiments, programming, working with numbers.	Strong problem-solving skills, good with abstract concepts and scientific thinking.
Spatial	Ability to visualize and manipulate objects in a spatial context.	Drawing, painting, designing, navigating, playing chess.	Good at visualizing, reading maps, and recognizing patterns.
Musical	Ability to recognize, create, and reproduce music and rhythm.	Playing instruments, singing, composing music, listening to music.	Good at understanding musical patterns, rhythms, and sounds.
Bodily-Kinesthetic	Ability to use the body skillfully and handle objects effectively.	Dancing, sports, acting, hands-on activities, building.	Good at physical coordination, handling tools, and expressing through movement.
Interpersonal	Ability to understand and interact effectively with others.	Group activities, teaching, counseling, mediating conflicts, socializing.	Strong communication skills, empathetic, good at building relationships.
Intrapersonal	Ability to understand oneself and use that knowledge to regulate one's own life.	Reflective activities, meditation, journaling, self-assessment.	Self-aware, good at self-regulation, understanding personal goals and motivations.
Naturalistic	Ability to recognize and categorize natural objects and processes.	Gardening, studying animals, exploring nature, environmental science.	Good at observing nature, understanding ecological relationships, and identifying flora and fauna.

Other Important Theories in Education

There are many different social, emotional, and learning theories in education. It is impossible to determine which theories you will be asked about on test day. However, the following theories are well-known in early childhood education.

These theories provide different lenses through which to understand human development and behavior, each emphasizing various factors such as unconscious processes, biological maturation, social interactions, and environmental influences.

PSYCHOANALYTIC THEORY

Proponent: Sigmund Freud

Overview:

- Psychoanalytic theory focuses on the influence of the unconscious mind on behavior.
- Freud's model of psychosexual development includes stages, each characterized by different conflicts that must be resolved for healthy psychological development.
- Erikson extended this theory with his psychosocial stages, emphasizing social relationships and spanning the entire lifespan. Each stage is marked by a specific conflict (e.g., trust vs. mistrust, autonomy vs. shame and doubt).

Key Concepts:

- Unconscious Mind: Contains thoughts, memories, and desires outside of conscious awareness.
- Defense Mechanisms: Strategies used by the ego to protect itself from anxiety and conflict.
- Stages of Development: Both Freud's psychosexual stages and Erikson's psychosocial stages outline key periods in development.

MATURATIONAL THEORY

Proponent: Arnold Gesell

Overview:

- Maturational theory posits that development is largely driven by genetics and biological maturation.
- Emphasizes the role of predetermined biological sequences in physical and cognitive development.
- Suggests that children will naturally develop certain abilities as they mature, with minimal influence from the environment.

Key Concepts:

- Genetic Predisposition: Development is pre-programmed by genetic factors.
- Developmental Milestones: Children reach physical and cognitive milestones in a predictable sequence.
- Readiness: Learning is most effective when a child is developmentally ready.

SOCIOCULTURAL THEORY

Proponent: Lev Vygotsky

Overview:

- Sociocultural theory emphasizes the role of social interaction and cultural context in cognitive development.
- Proposes that learning is a collaborative process, with children acquiring knowledge through guided interactions with more knowledgeable others (e.g., parents and teachers).
- Introduces the concept of the Zone of Proximal Development (ZPD), which represents tasks a child can perform with assistance but not yet independently.

Key Concepts:

- Social Interaction: Crucial for cognitive development.
- Cultural Tools: Language, symbols, and artifacts that shape thinking.
- Zone of Proximal Development (ZPD): The difference between what a learner can do independently and what they can achieve with guidance.

BEHAVIORAL THEORY

Proponent: B.F. Skinner, John B. Watson, and Ivan Pavlov

Overview:

- Behavioral theory focuses on observable behaviors and the ways they are learned through interactions with the environment.
- Emphasizes the role of reinforcement and punishment in shaping behavior.
- Includes classical conditioning (Pavlov) and operant conditioning (Skinner).

Key Concepts:

- Classical Conditioning: Learning through association, as demonstrated by Pavlov's experiments with dogs.
- Operant Conditioning: Learning through consequences, with behaviors reinforced by rewards or diminished by punishments.
- Behavior Modification: Techniques based on behavioral principles to change behavior.

Child Development and Learning – Practice Questions

1. Ms. Rivera notices that one of her students, Liam, struggles with fine motor skills and often avoids activities that require using scissors or writing. She wants to support his development in this area. Which of the following strategies would be most effective for Ms. Rivera to use to help Liam improve his fine motor skills?

   A. Assign Liam extra homework that focuses on writing practice.

   B. Incorporate activities such as playdough manipulation and beading into daily classroom activities.

   C. Pair Liam with a peer who excels in fine motor tasks and ask them to complete assignments together.

   D. Reduce the number of fine motor activities to avoid frustrating Liam.

2. During a group activity, Ms. Chen observes that several students are not participating and seem disengaged. She wants to ensure all students are motivated and involved. What is the best approach for Ms. Chen to take to increase student engagement during group activities?

   A. Reward the most active participants with extra recess time.

   B. Allow students to choose their own groups and activities.

   C. Assign specific roles to each student within the group based on their interests and strengths.

   D. Reduce the length of group activities to maintain interest.

3. Ms. Thompson notices that one of her students, Maria, often isolates herself during free play and seems hesitant to join her peers. Ms. Thompson wants to support Maria in developing her social skills. What strategy should Ms. Thompson use to help Maria become more socially engaged?

   A. Encourage Maria to play alone until she feels comfortable.

   B. Direct Maria to join a group activity without prior preparation.

   C. Facilitate a small group activity that includes Maria and a few friendly peers.

   D. Pair Maria with the most outgoing student in the class.

4. Ms. Parker is planning a week-long unit on animals for her 1st-grade class. She wants to use a holistic approach to ensure she addresses her students' cognitive, social, emotional, physical, and language needs. Which of the following plans best demonstrates Ms. Parker's use of a holistic approach in teaching the unit on animals?

   A. Read various books about animals and ask students to write a report on their favorite animal.

   B. Show animal documentaries and have students complete worksheets about animal habitats.

   C. Give a series of lectures on different types of animals and assign nightly homework to reinforce the concepts taught.

   D. Incorporate interactive activities such as group discussions about animal care, creating animal crafts, and a role-play activity.

5. Mr. Thompson's classroom includes students from various cultural backgrounds and abilities. He aims to create an inclusive environment where every student feels valued and supported.

   Which of the following strategies best reflects Mr. Thompson's commitment to fostering an inclusive classroom?

   A. Assigning the same tasks to all students for the purpose of equity and grading the students' performance.

   B. Creating culturally relevant lesson plans, providing differentiated instruction, and using assistive technologies for students with disabilities.

   C. Organizing students into homogeneous groups based on their abilities and cultural backgrounds.

   D. Minimizing group work to reduce potential conflicts and focusing on individual assignments.

6. Mr. Thompson notices that many students have difficulty focusing on their schoolwork and seem anxious and restless. Upon further investigation, he finds several students come to school without breakfast and live in unstable housing conditions. According to Maslow's hierarchy of needs, which level of needs is most likely unmet for Mr. Thompson's students, and how should he address this issue to improve their focus and learning?

   A. Physiological needs – He should ensure students have access to meals and a stable physical environment.

   B. Esteem needs – He should provide more opportunities for students to receive recognition and build self-confidence.

   C. Safety needs – He should implement a strict behavior management system to create a more structured environment.

   D. Love and belonging needs – He should focus on creating a strong sense of community and peer relationships in the classroom.

7. Ms. Lopez is a first-grade teacher observing her students during a science activity where they are asked to pour water from a tall, narrow container into a short, wide container. She notices that several students believe there is now less water in the short, wide container despite it being the same amount. Based on Piaget's stages of cognitive development, which stage are Ms. Lopez's students likely in, and what characteristic of that stage explains their belief?

   A. Sensorimotor stage – They rely solely on sensory experiences to understand the world.

   B. Preoperational stage – They struggle with the concept of conservation and focus on the appearance of the containers.

   C. Concrete operational stage – They use logical thinking but still make errors in judgment.

   D. Formal operational stage – They are beginning to use abstract reasoning but are not yet accurate in their observations.

8. Ms. Jackson is starting a new year as a second-grade teacher. While looking over her roster, she discovers three of her students are in special education and have Individualized Education Plans (IEPs). What should Ms. Jackson do to ensure she complies with federal law concerning these students? Choose **ALL** that apply.

   ☐ A. Carefully read and understand the student's IEP to become familiar with the specific goals, accommodations, modifications, and services outlined.

   ☐ B. Ensure that all accommodations and modifications specified in the IEP are implemented in the classroom.

   ☐ C. Maintain open communication with the special education teacher, parents, and other IEP team members.

   ☐ D. Modify the IEP to include new goals when students meet expectations and advance academically.

   ☐ E. Implement only the accommodations that fit the classroom setting and ignore those that do not.

9. Ms. Taylor is observing her kindergarten class in the classroom and during recess. She notices one of her students, Emma, engaging in various activities. Which of the following descriptions of physical development is typical for Emma, who is five years old?

   A. Emma hops on one foot, uses scissors to cut out shapes, and begins to draw more detailed pictures.

   B. Emma walks on tiptoe, starts to draw simple shapes, and throws a ball with one hand.

   C. Emma stacks blocks, runs steadily, and uses a crayon to scribble randomly.

   D. Emma jumps with both feet together, begins to dress herself with some help, and scribbles with a pencil.

10. Which of the following scenarios demonstrates a second-grade teacher using a constructivist approach in a science class?

    A. The teacher explains to the students that plants need sunlight to grow and shows them a video about photosynthesis.

    B. The teacher lectures on the parts of a plant and then asks the students to label a plant diagram in their notebooks.

    C. The teacher assigns a textbook chapter on plant life cycles for the students to read, and then they complete a worksheet with questions about the chapter.

    D. The teacher provides seeds, soil, and containers for the students to plant seeds and observe their growth.

Child Development and Learning – Answer Explanations

Number	Answer	Explanation
1.	B	**Correct Answer B:** Activities like manipulating playdough and beading are effective for developing fine motor skills in a fun and engaging way. These activities allow Liam to build strength and coordination in his hands through play, making it more likely that he will participate and improve. **Incorrect Answer A:** Assigning extra homework might not be engaging and could increase frustration. **Incorrect Answer C:** Pairing with a peer might not directly address his individual need. **Incorrect Answer A:** Reducing fine motor activities would not help him develop the necessary skills.
2.	C	**Correct Answer C:** Assigning specific roles can help each student feel valued and involved, leveraging their interests and strengths to keep them engaged. This approach promotes a sense of responsibility and cooperation. **Incorrect Answer A:** Rewarding only active participants can discourage less confident students. **Incorrect Answer B:** Allowing students to choose groups might not ensure balanced participation. **Incorrect Answer D:** Reducing activity length doesn't address the root cause of disengagement.
3.	C	**Correct Answer C:** Facilitating a small group activity with friendly peers can provide a comfortable and supportive environment for Maria to interact and build her social skills. A small, structured group activity is more likely to foster positive social interactions and gradual integration. **Incorrect Answer A:** Encouraging her to play alone does not address her social needs. **Incorrect Answer B:** Directing her to join a group without preparation may cause anxiety. **Incorrect Answer D:** Pairing her with the most outgoing student could be overwhelming.
4.	D	**Correct Answer D:** This option addresses multiple developmental areas: cognitive (learning about animals), social (group discussions), emotional (caring for animals), physical (creating crafts, role-playing), and language (discussing and presenting information). It provides a comprehensive, engaging, and interactive learning experience that meets the needs of the whole child. The other options do not offer multiple development areas.

Number	Answer	Explanation
5.	B	**Correct Answer B:** This approach acknowledges and supports the diverse needs and backgrounds of students, fostering an inclusive environment. **Incorrect Answer A:** This strategy does not consider individual needs and abilities, which can lead to some students being unfairly disadvantaged. **Incorrect Answer C:** This approach can reinforce stereotypes and limit students' opportunities to learn from diverse perspectives. **Incorrect Answer D:** Avoiding group work can prevent students from developing important social skills and learning to collaborate with peers from different backgrounds.
6.	A	**Correct Answer A:** Physiological needs – According to Maslow's hierarchy of needs, physiological needs are the most basic and must be met before students can focus on higher-level needs such as safety, belonging, esteem, and self-actualization. Addressing issues such as hunger and unstable housing by providing access to meals and a supportive physical environment will help students meet their basic needs, thereby improving their ability to focus and learn in the classroom. **Incorrect Answer B:** Esteem needs – While important, esteem needs are higher in the hierarchy and cannot be adequately addressed if basic physiological needs are unmet. **Incorrect Answer C:** Safety needs – Though safety is crucial, the immediate issue of hunger and unstable housing pertains more directly to physiological needs. **Incorrect Answer D:** Love and belonging needs – While fostering a sense of community is important, the primary issue is meeting the students' basic physiological needs for food and stable housing.
7.	B	**Correct Answer B:** Preoperational stage – This stage is characterized by difficulty understanding that quantity remains the same despite changes in shape or appearance. **Incorrect Answer A:** Sensorimotor stage – This stage pertains to infants and toddlers who rely on sensory experiences and motor actions to understand the world, which does not apply to the described scenario. **Incorrect Answer C:** Concrete operational stage – Students in this stage (ages 7-11) typically understand conservation, which contradicts the described behavior. **Incorrect Answer D:** Formal operational stage – This stage involves abstract reasoning and logical thinking, which is beyond the typical developmental stage of first-grade students.

Number	Answer	Explanation
8.	A, B & C	**Correct Answer A:** This ensures specific needs and supports required for each student, which is a legal obligation under the Individuals with Disabilities Education Act (IDEA). **Correct Answer B:** This ensures the teacher is compliant with federal law, which mandates that all accommodations and modifications specified in an IEP must be implemented as outlined. **Correct Answer C:** This ensures collaboration and communication with the IEP team, which is crucial for monitoring the student's progress and making any necessary adjustments to their educational plan. **Incorrect Answer D:** Modifying an IEP is a decision that must be made by the entire IEP team, including the parents and special education professionals, during a formal IEP meeting. Ms. Jackson alone cannot unilaterally make changes to the IEP. **Incorrect Answer E:** It is illegal and unethical to selectively implement accommodations. All accommodations and modifications specified in the IEP must be followed to ensure the student's rights and educational needs are fully met.
9.	A	**Correct Answer A:** At ages 5-6, children typically develop better coordination and fine motor skills. Hopping on one foot, using scissors to cut out shapes, and drawing more detailed pictures are typical physical development milestones for this age group. The other options describe skills more appropriate for younger children. **Incorrect Answer B:** These activities are more typical for a younger child. **Incorrect Answer C:** These activities are also more typical for younger children. **Incorrect Answer D:** While these are developmentally appropriate activities, they do not reflect the more advanced skills typical of a five-year-old.
10.	D	**Correct Answer D:** In a constructivist approach, learning is facilitated through hands-on activities and inquiry-based experiences, allowing students to build their own understanding. **Incorrect Answer A:** This approach is more teacher-centered and does not engage students in active learning. **Incorrect Answer B:** This method is more traditional and does not involve the students in hands-on, experiential learning. **Incorrect Answer C:** This approach is also more passive and does not align with the principles of constructivist learning.

II. Observation, Documentation, and Assessment

Teaching and learning are intertwined in a continuous cycle. Teachers set learning objectives, design classroom activities, and evaluate the results. Highly effective teachers do this to measure the effectiveness of their teaching as it relates to student learning. After each evaluation, teachers set new objectives based on the assessment outcomes, creating a perpetual loop of learning and evaluation.

Teachers must understand and use different assessment tools to ensure assessments align with teaching objectives, activities, and the curriculum. Additionally, teachers must effectively communicate assessment information to families and other professionals.

The following concepts are discussed in this content category:

- Assessment Methods in Early Childhood Education
- Responsible Assessment Practices to Meet the Diverse Needs of Children
- Screening, Referral, and Evaluation
- Communicating Assessment Results with Families and Community

Assessment Methods in Early Childhood Education

Understanding and effectively utilizing various assessment methods can help educators enhance their instructional practices, support student learning, and create a responsive and dynamic classroom environment.

Goals, Benefits, and Uses of Assessment

Being a data-driven early childhood educator is crucial because it enables teachers to make informed decisions that enhance young children's learning experiences and outcomes. Educators can identify individual strengths and areas needing improvement by systematically collecting and analyzing data on student performance, behavior, and development, allowing for personalized instruction that meets each child's unique needs.

Data-driven practices help teachers monitor progress, adjust teaching strategies, and implement timely interventions, ensuring that every child is on a path to success. Furthermore, using data to guide instruction fosters accountability. It provides a solid foundation for communicating with parents and stakeholders about a child's growth and educational needs, ultimately supporting a more effective and responsive early childhood education environment.

Quick Tip

The only reason to use assessment is to make instructional decisions. Putting grades in the gradebook does little to help students achieve. However, using assessment data to scaffold instruction and intervene when necessary will help increase student outcomes.

Qualitative vs Quantitative Data

In the early childhood classroom, combining qualitative and quantitative data provides a holistic view of each child, ensuring that instructional strategies and interventions are effective and tailored to meet individual needs. For instance, a teacher might use quantitative data from a phonics test to identify students who need help with specific skills and then use qualitative observations to understand how those students engage with phonics activities during class.

Qualitative Data:

- **Definition**: Qualitative data is descriptive and involves characteristics that cannot me quantified with numbers. It provides insights into the quality and nature of a child's behavior, interactions, and learning processes.

- **Examples in Assessments**:

  - **Observations**: Documenting a child's social interactions, problem-solving approaches, and activity engagement.

  - **Anecdotal Records**: Writing detailed notes on specific incidents or patterns of behavior.

  - **Portfolios**: Collecting samples of a child's work, such as drawings, writing samples, projects, and teacher notes.

- **Usage**: Qualitative data helps educators understand the context of a child's development and learning. It provides a deeper insight into a child's strengths, interests, and areas needing support, which can guide personalized instruction and intervention strategies.

Quick Tip

Anecdotal records are notes the teacher writes down during observations. They are qualitative data that outline what a student can do. These notes can be shared with parents during conferences.

Quantitative Data:

- **Definition**: Quantitative data is numerical and provides measurable evidence of a child's performance and progress.

- **Examples in Assessments**:

  - **Standardized Tests**: Scores from literacy and numeracy assessments.

  - **Checklists and Rating Scales**: Counting the number of times a child demonstrates a specific skill or behavior.

  - **Attendance Records**: Tracking the days a child is present or absent.

- **Usage**: Quantitative data allows educators to compare a child's performance against benchmarks or norms. It provides objective evidence of a child's academic progress, skill development, and areas needing additional focus. This data is essential for tracking growth over time and making data-driven decisions.

Goals of Assessment:

- **Inform Instruction**: To gather student learning and development data to tailor instruction to meet individual needs.

- **Monitor Progress**: To track student progress over time and identify areas of strength and areas needing improvement.

- **Identify Needs**: To detect learning disabilities, developmental delays, or giftedness, ensuring appropriate interventions or enrichment.

- **Accountability**: To ensure educational standards are met and to provide accountability for educators and programs.

Benefits of Assessment:

- **Personalized Learning**: Helps in designing instruction that meets the unique needs of each student.
- **Early Intervention**: Identifies issues early, allowing for timely interventions to mitigate learning and developmental delays.
- **Enhanced Teaching**: Provides teachers with insights into effective teaching strategies and areas for professional development.
- **Engagement**: Involves students in their learning process, fostering self-assessment and goal setting.

Uses of Assessment:

- **Curriculum Planning**: Informs the development and adjustment of curriculum to ensure it meets the needs of all students.
- **Instructional Strategies**: Guides the selection of teaching methods and materials based on student needs and learning styles.
- **Communication with Stakeholders**: Provides a basis for communicating progress and needs with parents, administrators, and other educators.

Incorporating a Variety of Assessment Methods

The following are common assessment types used in the early childhood classroom. This is not an exhaustive list, but it does provide an overview of the main types of assessments used in public education.

Formal Assessments:

- **Definition**: Structured, standardized tests that measure specific outcomes.
- **Examples**: Standardized tests, quizzes, and end-of-unit exams.
- **Use**: Provides comparative data across different populations and benchmarks against standards.

Informal Assessments:

- **Definition**: Unstructured, observational methods to gauge student learning.
- **Examples**: Observations, checklists, anecdotal records, student work samples.
- **Use**: Offers real-time insights into student progress and classroom dynamics.

Standardized Assessments:

- **Definition**: Tests administered and scored consistently.
- **Examples**: State assessments and nationally normed tests.
- **Use**: Ensures consistency and reliability in measuring student performance against broader benchmarks.

Formative Assessments:

- **Definition**: Ongoing assessments used to monitor student learning.
- **Examples**: Exit tickets, think-pair-share, and in-class activities.
- **Use**: Provides immediate feedback to adjust instruction and support student learning.

Summative Assessments:

- **Definition**: Evaluations at the end of an instructional period to measure student learning or outcomes.
- **Examples**: Final exams, end-of-term projects, and performance tasks.
- **Use**: Assesses overall student achievement and program effectiveness.

Observation, Documentation, and Assessment

Advantages and Disadvantages of Assessment Methods

Assessment Method	Advantages	Disadvantages
Formal Assessments	Provides quantifiable data; standardization allows for comparison.	Can be stressful for students; may not capture all aspects of learning.
Informal Assessments	Flexible and adaptable; provides immediate feedback; can be integrated into daily activities.	Subjective; may lack consistency and reliability; harder to compare across students.
Standardized Assessments	Offers reliability and validity; provides benchmarks for comparison.	Can narrow curriculum focus; may not account for individual differences; high-stakes nature can cause stress.
Formative Assessments	Encourages ongoing feedback and adjustment; supports student learning in real-time.	Time-consuming for teachers to implement continuously; may be perceived as less formal.
Summative Assessments	Provides a clear measure of student achievement at the end of a period; useful for final evaluations.	May not reflect ongoing learning process; can be high-stakes and stressful.

Collecting Data:

- **Systematic Observations**: Use structured observation protocols to gather consistent data.
- **Checklists and Rubrics**: Employ tools to ensure comprehensive coverage of skills and competencies.
- **Portfolios**: Compile student work to provide a holistic view of progress.

Analyzing Data:

- **Quantitative Analysis**: Use statistical methods to interpret numerical data from assessments.
- **Qualitative Analysis**: Examine patterns and themes in observational notes and student work.
- **Comparative Analysis**: Compare results across different student groups or against benchmarks.

Interpreting Data:

- **Contextual Understanding**: Consider the context of assessments, such as the learning environment and student backgrounds.
- **Triangulation**: Use multiple data sources to confirm findings and provide a more accurate picture.
- **Actionable Insights**: Focus on deriving insights that can inform instructional adjustments and targeted interventions.

Informing Instructional Decision-Making:

- **Individualized Instruction**: Tailor teaching strategies to meet the diverse needs of students based on assessment data.
- **Group Instruction**: Use assessment results to form groups for differentiated instruction.

- **Curriculum Adjustments**: Modify curriculum content and pacing based on overall class performance and specific learning gaps.
- **Professional Development**: Identify areas where teachers may need additional training or resources to support student learning.

The following table provides an overview of different types of assessments used in early childhood education, helping educators select appropriate methods to evaluate and support student learning.

Assessment Type	Definition	Examples
Formative	Ongoing assessments used to monitor student learning and provide feedback for instructional adjustments.	Observations, exit tickets, think-pair-share, daily quizzes, and anecdotal records.
Summative	Evaluations at the end of an instructional period to measure student learning against specific criteria.	End-of-unit tests, final projects, standardized tests, and cumulative assessments.
Criterion-Referenced	Assessments that measure student performance against a fixed set of criteria or learning standards.	State assessments, benchmark tests, and teacher-created tests based on curriculum standards.
Norm-Referenced	Assessments that compare a student's performance to a norm group, typically representative of the population.	Standardized tests like the SAT, IQ tests, and national percentile rankings.
Performance-Based	Assessments that require students to demonstrate their knowledge and skills through practical tasks.	Science experiments, presentations, role-playing, and art projects.
Portfolio	A collection of student work that demonstrates learning progress, achievements, and abilities over time.	Writing samples, artwork, recordings of oral presentations, and reflective journals.
Universal Screening	Brief assessments administered to all students to identify those who may need additional support or interventions.	Reading fluency tests, math skill screenings, and developmental checklists.

Diagnostic Assessments

A diagnostic assessment is a form of pre-assessment that helps educators identify students' existing knowledge, skills, strengths, and areas of need before instruction begins. It is used to diagnose specific learning difficulties, developmental delays, or gaps in understanding to develop targeted interventions and personalized learning plans. Diagnostic assessments are typically administered at the beginning of a learning period and are crucial for tailoring instruction to meet the diverse needs of young learners.

Example of Diagnostic Assessment in Early Childhood Education

Ms. Rivera is a kindergarten teacher who wants to understand her students' literacy skills at the start of the school year. She administers a diagnostic assessment that includes several tasks:

1. **Letter Recognition**: Ms. Rivera shows each child a series of uppercase and lowercase letters and asks them to identify as many as possible.

2. **Phonemic Awareness**: She asks the children to identify the beginning sounds of words, such as identifying the "b" sound at the start of "ball."

3. **Word Recognition**: Ms. Rivera presents a list of simple sight words (e.g., "the," "and," "cat") and asks the children to read them aloud.

4. **Story Retelling**: She reads a short story to the children and then asks them to retell it in their own words, checking for comprehension and vocabulary use.

Based on the results of this diagnostic assessment, Ms. Rivera identifies which children are struggling with letter recognition, phonemic awareness, word recognition, and comprehension. She uses this information to create small groups for targeted instruction and develop individualized learning plans that address each child's specific needs, ensuring that all students receive the support they need to develop their literacy skills.

Quick Tip

Teachers can use a diagnostic assessment to identify students' specific deficits in any area. For example, after a universal screening for general reading, the teacher can administer a diagnostic assessment to collect even more data on individual reading skills—phonological awareness, phonics, fluency, etc.—so the teacher can plan instruction and intervene most effectively.

Responsible Assessment Practices to Meet the Diverse Needs of Children

Understanding how to apply responsible assessment practices is crucial for meeting the diverse needs of children in early childhood education. This includes children who are culturally and linguistically diverse, those with disabilities, and those with exceptionalities. Responsible assessment practices ensure that all children are evaluated fairly and accurately, allowing educators to provide appropriate support and instruction.

The following information outlines the key principles of responsible assessment and examples and scenarios of what that looks like in an early childhood classroom.

Key Principles of Responsible Assessment

Cultural and Linguistic Responsiveness:

- **Understand Cultural Contexts**: Be aware of students' cultural backgrounds and values. Use assessment tools that are culturally sensitive and avoid bias.

- **Language Considerations**: Assessments should accommodate linguistically diverse students' language proficiency. This may involve using bilingual assessments or providing instructions in the child's home language when possible.

- **Family Involvement**: Engage with families to gain a better understanding of the child's cultural and linguistic background. This can provide valuable context for interpreting assessment results.

Inclusive Practices for Students with Disabilities:

- **Universal Design for Learning (UDL)**: Implement UDL principles in assessments to ensure they are accessible to all students. This includes providing multiple means of representation, expression, and engagement.

- **Accommodations and Modifications**: Use appropriate accommodations (e.g., extended time, alternate formats) and modifications to ensure that assessments accurately reflect the abilities of students with disabilities.

- **Individualized Education Program (IEP) Considerations**: Align assessments with the goals and objectives outlined in each student's IEP and collaborate with special education professionals to interpret and use the assessment data effectively.

Addressing the Needs of Exceptional Students:

- **Differentiated Assessment**: Tailor assessments to meet the unique strengths and needs of students with exceptionalities. This includes both gifted students and those who may need additional support.

- **Challenging and Enriching**: Provide assessments that challenge gifted students and allow them to demonstrate their advanced skills and knowledge. This might include open-ended questions, higher-order thinking tasks, and opportunities for creative expression.

- **Multiple Measures**: Use a variety of assessment methods to capture a comprehensive picture of a student's abilities. This includes formative, summative, performance-based, and portfolio assessments.

Examples of Practical Application of Responsible Assessment Practices

Culturally and Linguistically Diverse Students:

- Scenario: A teacher is assessing a bilingual student's reading skills.

- Responsible Practice: Use bilingual reading assessments and allow the student to demonstrate comprehension in both languages. Engage with the student's family to understand their literacy practices at home and incorporate culturally relevant materials.

Students with Disabilities:

- Scenario: A student with a visual impairment is taking a math test.

- Responsible Practice: Provide the test in Braille or use a screen reader. Allow additional time and ensure that manipulatives or other tactile resources are available. Collaborate with the special education team to interpret results accurately.

Exceptional Students:

- Scenario: A gifted student finishes assignments quickly and correctly but seems bored.

- Responsible Practice: Provide assessments that include higher-level thinking tasks, such as project-based learning opportunities or complex problem-solving activities. Use these assessments to identify areas where the student can be further challenged and enriched.

Quick Tip

When designing and implementing assessments, always consider the unique backgrounds and needs of each student. Use various assessment methods to capture a complete picture of their abilities and ensure fairness and accessibility. Remember to engage with families and collaborate with specialists to gain deeper insights and provide the best support for every child.

Screening, Referral, and Evaluation

As an active participant in the screening, referral, and evaluation process, teachers play a critical role in identifying and supporting students who may need additional services or interventions. This involvement is crucial for ensuring that all students receive the appropriate resources to meet their educational and developmental needs. Understanding this role helps teachers effectively contribute to the process and advocate for their students.

SCREENING

Screening involves using brief assessments to identify students who may be at risk for developmental delays, learning disabilities, or other challenges.

Teacher's Role:

1. **Conducting Screenings**: Administer initial screening tools and assessments to all students to identify those needing further evaluation.

2. **Observing and Documenting**: Observe students' behavior, academic performance, and social interactions. Document any concerns or deviations from typical developmental milestones.

3. **Using Multiple Measures**: Utilize a variety of screening tools and methods to gather comprehensive information about a student's abilities and needs.

Best Practices:

- Be consistent and unbiased when administering screenings.
- Use culturally and linguistically appropriate tools.
- Communicate with families about the purpose and results of screenings.

REFERRAL

Referral is directing a student to specialized services or further evaluation based on the initial screening results or observed needs.

Teacher's Role:

1. **Identifying Concerns**: Recognize signs that a student may need additional support based on screening results and classroom observations.

2. **Initiating Referrals**: Complete referral forms and provide detailed documentation to support the need for further evaluation. Include information on the student's strengths, challenges, and any interventions already attempted.

3. **Collaborating with Families**: Discuss concerns with the student's family, explaining the referral process and the reasons for the referral. Obtain parental consent as needed.

Best Practices:

- Ensure referrals are timely to avoid delays in support.
- Maintain confidentiality and handle sensitive information with care.
- Provide families with resources and support during the referral process.

EVALUATION

Evaluation involves a comprehensive assessment conducted by specialists to determine a student's specific needs and eligibility for special education services or other interventions.

Teacher's Role:

1. **Providing Input**: Share observations, screening results, and relevant classroom data with the evaluation team. Offer insights into students' academic performance, behavior, and social interactions.

2. **Participating in Meetings**: Attend evaluation meetings and Individualized Education Program (IEP) team meetings to discuss findings and contribute to developing intervention plans.

3. **Implementing Recommendations**: Work collaboratively with specialists to integrate recommended strategies and accommodations into the classroom. Monitor the student's progress and adjust instruction as needed.

Best Practices:

- Stay informed about the evaluation process and criteria.

- Engage in ongoing professional development to better understand various disabilities and intervention strategies.

- Foster a collaborative relationship with special education staff, specialists, and families.

Teachers are vital in screening, referral, and evaluation, ensuring students receive timely and appropriate support. By actively participating in these processes, teachers help create an inclusive and responsive educational environment that addresses the diverse needs of all students. Understanding these roles and responsibilities is essential for effective advocacy and intervention in early childhood education.

Statement of Behavior vs. Interference

Understanding the difference between a statement of behavior and inference is crucial for accurate and unbiased assessment and observation in educational settings. When teachers observe behavior, they should do so objectively and without bias.

A statement of behavior outlines what the student is doing without adding any interpretations or extra insights. In contrast, interference involves drawing conclusions from the observation that may or may not be accurate. Interferences can often hinder true data collection and lead to biased assessments.

Statement of Behavior:

- **Definition**: This involves objectively describing what is directly seen or heard without adding interpretation or assumptions.

- **Example**: "Johnny raised his hand and waited for the teacher to call on him before speaking."

- **Characteristics**:
    - Factual and specific
    - Free of personal bias or interpretation
    - Directly verifiable

Interference:

- **Definition**: This involves making a conclusion or interpretation based on the observed behavior, which may include assumptions about motives, feelings, or underlying reasons.

- **Example**: "Johnny raised his hand because he is eager to participate in class."

- **Characteristics**:
  - Includes personal interpretation or assumptions
  - Goes beyond what is directly observable
  - Not directly verifiable without further evidence

Quick Tip

Multi-Tiered System of Supports (MTSS) is a comprehensive, data-driven framework designed to meet the academic, behavioral, and social-emotional needs of all students through a layered approach of increasingly intensive interventions. MTSS integrates assessment and intervention within a multi-level prevention system to maximize student outcomes. It involves continuous monitoring of student progress, data-based decision making, and evidence-based practices to provide support that is responsive to the needs of every student. We will cover MTSS in-depth in subsequent sections of the study guide.

Communicating Assessment Results with Families and Community

Effective communication of assessment results with families and the community is a crucial aspect of early childhood education. It involves sharing information about a child's progress, strengths, and areas needing improvement in a clear, understandable, and respectful manner. This communication helps to build a collaborative relationship between educators, families, and community members, ensuring that everyone is working together to support the child's development and learning. It also involves using various methods, such as written reports, parent-teacher conferences, and community meetings, to convey assessment data and discuss strategies for supporting the child's growth.

Classroom Scenario: Preschool

Ms. Williams, a preschool teacher, has recently conducted a series of assessments to evaluate her students' cognitive, social, emotional, and physical development. She needs to communicate the results to the families and the community effectively.

Action Steps:

1. **Parent-Teacher Conferences**: Ms. Williams schedules individual meetings with each child's parents to discuss the assessment results. During these conferences, she uses simple language and visual aids, such as charts and graphs, to explain the child's progress and areas needing attention. She also listens to parents' observations and concerns, creating a two-way dialogue.

2. **Written Reports**: Ms. Williams prepares detailed written reports summarizing the assessment findings for each child. These reports include specific examples of the child's work and behavior, as well as personalized recommendations for activities and strategies that parents can use at home to support their child's development.

3. **Community Meeting**: Ms. Williams organizes a community meeting to share general trends and findings from the assessments with the broader community, including other educators and community stakeholders. She highlights successful strategies and areas where additional community support or resources may be beneficial. She removes individual students' identifying information for confidentiality purposes.

4. **Follow-Up**: Ms. Williams ensures ongoing communication by providing regular updates on each child's progress and arranging follow-up meetings with parents as needed. She also encourages parents to reach out with any questions or concerns, fostering an environment of continuous collaboration and support.

Outcome: By effectively communicating the assessment results, Ms. Williams helps parents and the community understand each child's development and engage in meaningful ways to support their growth. This collaborative approach ensures that children receive comprehensive support both at school and at home, enhancing their overall development and learning experiences.

This page intentionally left blank.

1. Ms. Lopez notices that some kindergarten students struggle to recognize letter sounds. She decides to use an assessment method that will help her monitor their progress daily and adjust her teaching strategies accordingly. Which type of assessment would best suit Ms. Lopez's goal?

   A. Summative Assessment

   B. Norm-Referenced Assessment

   C. Formative Assessment

   D. Portfolio Assessment

2. Mr. Johnson is preparing to evaluate his first-grade students at the end of the school year to determine how well they have met the learning objectives outlined in the curriculum.

   Which type of assessment should Mr. Johnson use to measure his students' overall achievement and compare their performance against set standards?

   A. Criterion-Referenced Assessment

   B. Formative Assessment

   C. Performance-Based Assessment

   D. Universal Screening

3. Ms. Brown wants to understand how her preschool students' language development compares to other students in the state. She plans to use an assessment method that will provide her with this comparative data. Which type of assessment should Ms. Brown use to achieve her goal?

   A. Performance-Based Assessment

   B. Norm-Referenced Assessment

   C. Portfolio Assessment

   D. Summative Assessment

4. Ms. Nguyen is preparing to assess her class of diverse kindergarten students, including several English Language Learners (ELLs). She wants to ensure her assessments accurately reflect each student's knowledge and skills without being biased by their language proficiency.

   Which of the following assessment practices would best help Ms. Nguyen achieve this goal?

   A. Administer a standardized test in English to all students and compare their scores.

   B. Use bilingual assessments and provide instructions in the students' home languages.

   C. Give extra time to ELL students to complete the same assessments as their peers.

   D. Ask ELL students to complete an oral exam in English to assess their comprehension.

5. Mr. Rodriguez is assessing his first-grade students, who include children with various learning disabilities. He wants to ensure that his assessments are inclusive and accurately reflect each student's abilities.

Which assessment practice should Mr. Rodriguez implement to meet the needs of his students with learning disabilities?

A. Use the same standard test for all students without any modifications

B. Give easier questions to students with disabilities to ensure they can succeed.

C. Exclude students with disabilities from the assessment to avoid skewing the results.

D. Allow students to use assistive technologies and provide additional time for the test.

6. Ms. Taylor is a kindergarten teacher who has noticed that one of her students, Jacob, is struggling with fine motor skills and social interactions. After documenting her observations, she decides to initiate the referral process.

Which of the following actions should Ms. Taylor take to initiate the referral process for Jacob effectively?

A. Discuss her concerns with Jacob's parents, provide them with her observations, and obtain their consent for further evaluation.

B. Complete a referral form and submit it to the school principal without discussing it with the parents.

C. Wait until the end of the school year to see if Jacob improves before making a referral.

D. Implement her own intervention strategies before consulting specialists.

7. Mr. Johnson, a first-grade teacher, is preparing for an upcoming evaluation meeting for one of his students, Lily, who has been referred for special education services. He wants to ensure that he provides valuable input during the meeting.

Which of the following actions should Mr. Johnson take to contribute effectively to Lily's evaluation process?

A. Share his classroom observations and detailed documentation of Lily's academic performance and behavior with the evaluation team.

B. Attend the meeting but refrain from providing input since the specialists will handle the evaluation.

C. Only share positive aspects of Lily's performance to avoid any negative bias.

D. Rely mostly on standardized test scores to provide the most accurate information about Lily's needs.

8. Ms. Davis, a preschool teacher, is preparing for a meeting with the family of a child who has recently undergone a developmental screening. The family is from a culturally diverse background and speaks primarily Spanish at home.

Which of the following strategies should Ms. Davis use to ensure effective communication and involvement of the family in the screening process?

A. Conduct the meeting in English and provide a written summary in Spanish afterward.

B. Use an interpreter during the meeting and provide translated materials in Spanish.

C. Ask the family to bring someone who can translate for them.

D. Conduct the meeting in English and rely on the child to translate key points to the family.

9. Mr. Johnson is working with a team to develop an Individualized Education Program (IEP) for a student with learning disabilities. He wants to ensure that the student's family is actively involved and that their input is considered throughout the process.

   Which of the following actions should Mr. Johnson take to establish effective collaboration with the family?

   A. Schedule the IEP meeting at a time convenient for the school staff.

   B. Provide the family with detailed reports but limit their involvement to avoid overwhelming them.

   C. Encourage the family to share their observations and goals for their child and ensure their input is integrated into the IEP.

   D. Rely solely on standardized test scores to determine the child's needs and goals.

10. Indicate how assessment results can be communicated to families effectively and provide guidelines to help parents understand how to use this information to support their children's learning. Select **ALL** that apply.

   ☐ A. Provide written reports with detailed explanations of assessment results and suggested activities for home support.

   ☐ B. Use educational jargon to ensure the communication sounds professional and authoritative.

   ☐ C. Hold face-to-face meetings or conferences to discuss assessment results and answer any questions the parents might have.

   ☐ D. Send home the raw data from assessments with minimum explanation.

   ☐ E. Provide visual aids, such as charts and graphs, to help explain the assessment results clearly.

   ☐ F. Offer workshops or informational sessions for parents to understand how to interpret assessment results and use them to support their child's learning.

Number	Answer	Explanation
1.	C	**Correct Answer C:** Formative assessments are designed to monitor student learning and provide ongoing feedback that can be used by teachers to improve their teaching and by students to improve their learning. Ms. Lopez's goal of monitoring progress daily and adjusting her teaching strategies accordingly aligns perfectly with the purpose of formative assessments. **Incorrect Answer A:** Summative assessments are typically used to evaluate student learning at the end of an instructional period by comparing it against some standard or benchmark. These assessments are not suited for daily monitoring and immediate instructional adjustments. **Incorrect Answer B:** Norm-referenced assessments compare a student's performance against a group, usually to rank students. These assessments do not provide the ongoing feedback necessary for daily instructional adjustments. **Incorrect Answer D:** While portfolio assessments can provide a comprehensive view of a student's progress over time, they are not typically used for daily monitoring and immediate instructional adjustments. They are more suitable for periodic review and reflection on a student's body of work.
2.	A	**Correct Answer A:** Criterion-referenced assessments measure a student's performance against a fixed set of standards or specific learning objectives. Mr. Johnson's goal is to determine how well his students have met the learning objectives outlined in the curriculum, making criterion-referenced assessment the most appropriate choice. **Incorrect Answer B:** Formative assessments are used to monitor student learning and provide ongoing feedback during the instructional process. They are not typically used to measure overall achievement at the end of the school year. **Incorrect Answer C:** Performance-based assessments require students to demonstrate their knowledge and skills through projects, presentations, or other tasks. While useful, they may not comprehensively measure overall achievement against set standards for all curriculum objectives. **Incorrect Answer D:** Universal screenings are brief assessments given to all students to identify those who may need additional support or interventions. They are not designed to measure overall achievement or compare student performance against curriculum standards at the end of the school year.

Number	Answer	Explanation
3.	B	**Correct Answer B:** Norm-referenced assessments compare a student's performance to that of a larger group, often resulting in a percentile ranking. This method will provide Ms. Brown with comparative data on her preschool students' language development relative to other students in the state, making it the best choice for her goal. **Incorrect Answer A:** Performance-based assessments evaluate students' skills and knowledge through practical tasks but do not provide comparative data against a larger group. This type of assessment would not help Ms. Brown understand how her students' language development compares to others. **Incorrect Answer C:** Portfolio assessments compile a collection of a student's work over time to show progress and development. While useful for individual student evaluation, they do not offer comparative data against other students' performances. **Incorrect Answer D:** Summative assessments evaluate student learning at the end of an instructional period and measure the extent to which learning objectives have been met. However, they do not provide comparative data relative to a larger group, which is what Ms. Brown is seeking.
4.	B	**Correct Answer B:** Bilingual assessments and instructions in students' home languages help ensure that language proficiency does not bias the evaluation of their knowledge and skills. This practice allows Ms. Nguyen to assess her ELL students more accurately. **Incorrect Answer A:** Standardized tests in English may not accurately reflect the knowledge and skills of ELL students, as their language proficiency can impact their performance. This approach may lead to biased results and does not accommodate the linguistic needs of diverse learners. **Incorrect Answer C:** While providing extra time can help ELL students, it does not address the core issue of language proficiency affecting their understanding of the test content. This practice does not ensure that the assessment accurately reflects their knowledge and skills. **Incorrect Answer D:** Oral exams in English for ELL students may not accurately measure their knowledge and skills if their English proficiency is limited. This method can still be biased by language proficiency, leading to an inaccurate assessment of their capabilities.
5.	D	**Correct Answer D:** This approach ensures that students with learning disabilities have the necessary accommodations to accurately demonstrate their abilities, promoting an inclusive assessment environment. **Incorrect Answer A:** This practice does not accommodate the diverse needs of students with learning disabilities, potentially resulting in inaccurate reflections of their abilities. **Incorrect Answer B:** Providing easier questions does not accurately assess the students' abilities or promote their academic growth. **Incorrect Answer C:** Excluding students with disabilities is discriminatory and fails to provide an inclusive assessment environment.

Number	Answer	Explanation
6.	A	**Correct Answer A:** This step is essential in the referral process, ensuring parental involvement and consent for further evaluation. **Incorrect Answer B:** Parental involvement is crucial in the referral process, and bypassing this step can lead to misunderstandings and lack of consent. **Incorrect Answer C:** Delaying the referral process may hinder timely intervention and support for Jacob. **Incorrect Answer D:** This approach lacks obtaining parental input, a critical step in the referral process.
7.	A	**Correct Answer A:** Providing comprehensive and detailed observations helps the evaluation team gain a complete understanding of Lily's needs and strengths. **Incorrect Answer B:** Active participation from the classroom teacher is essential for a holistic evaluation process. **Incorrect Answer C:** A balanced view, including both strengths and areas for improvement, is necessary for accurate evaluation. **Incorrect Answer D:** While standardized test scores are important, they should be complemented with classroom observations and other qualitative data.
8.	B	**Correct Answer B:** This approach ensures effective communication and involvement of the family, respecting their linguistic and cultural background. **Incorrect Answer A:** This method may not facilitate real-time understanding and engagement during the meeting. **Incorrect Answer C:** Relying on family-provided translators may not ensure professional and accurate translation. **Incorrect Answer D:** Using the child as a translator is inappropriate and can lead to misunderstandings.
9.	C	**Correct Answer C:** Active collaboration with the family ensures that the IEP reflects the child's needs and the family's perspectives. **Incorrect Answer A:** The meeting should be scheduled at a time convenient for the family to ensure their participation. **Incorrect Answer B:** Limiting family involvement does not promote a collaborative approach. **Incorrect Answer D:** A comprehensive approach, including family input, is essential for developing an effective IEP.

Number	Answer	Explanation
10.	A, C, E & F	**Correct Answer A:** Detailed reports help parents understand their child's progress and how to support learning at home.
		Correct Answer C: Personal interactions allow for in-depth discussions and clarification of assessment results.
		Correct Answer E: Visual aids enhance understanding by presenting data in an accessible format.
		Correct Answer F: Workshops provide parents with the tools to effectively use assessment information to support their child.
		Incorrect Answer B: Using jargon can confuse parents and hinder their understanding.
		Incorrect Answer D: Raw data without explanation is not useful to parents and does not support informed decision-making.

Observation, Documentation, and Assessment

This page intentionally left blank.

III. Developmentally Appropriate Practices

Developmentally appropriate practices (DAP) in the early childhood classroom are crucial for fostering a supportive, engaging, and effective learning environment. These practices involve teaching methods and educational activities based on young children's developmental stages and individual needs. By considering each child's age, developmental status, and cultural background, educators can create challenging and achievable learning experiences.

DAP encourages children to explore, experiment, and discover at their own pace, which promotes a deeper understanding and retention of knowledge. Additionally, these practices support children's social, emotional, physical, and cognitive development, laying a solid foundation for future learning and growth. Implementing developmentally appropriate practices ensures that all children feel valued, respected, and capable, which enhances their self-esteem and motivation to learn.

The following concepts are discussed in this section:

- Structuring the Classroom Environment to Support Children's Learning
- Applying a Flexible, Research-Based Repertoire of Teaching and Learning Approaches
- Designing a Classroom to Accommodate Students with Physical and Emotional Disabilities

Structuring the Classroom Environment to Support Children's Learning

Creating an effective learning environment in an early childhood classroom involves several key components. These components help ensure that the physical space, daily routines, and instructional strategies are all aligned to support the diverse needs of young learners.

1. Organizing the Physical Configuration

A well-organized physical classroom environment can significantly enhance children's learning experiences. Here are some strategies to consider:

- **Learning Centers**: Create designated areas within the classroom where children can engage in specific types of activities. Common centers include a reading corner, a math station, an art area, and a science exploration table. These centers should be clearly defined and equipped with the necessary materials to support the learning goals for each subject area.
- **Accessibility and Safety**: Ensure that all materials are accessible to children and that the classroom is arranged to provide safe movement. Low shelves, labeled bins, and child-sized furniture can help children find and use materials independently.
- **Flexibility**: Design the space to be flexible, allowing for reconfiguration based on planned activities. Movable furniture and open floor space can accommodate individual work and group activities.

2. Establishing Schedules and Routines

Consistent schedules and routines are vital for creating a stable and predictable environment where children feel secure and ready to learn.

- **Daily Schedule**: Develop a daily schedule that balances various activities, including large group instruction, small group work, independent play, and outdoor time. Visual schedules can help children understand and anticipate the sequence of events throughout the day.
- **Routine Activities**: Establish routines for common classroom activities, such as arrival and departure, transitioning between activities, and clean-up times. These routines help children develop self-regulation and independence.

- **Consistency**: Maintain consistency in schedules and routines to help children feel more comfortable and focused. However, be flexible enough to adjust as needed based on the dynamics of the day and the children's individual needs.

3. Matching Learning Configurations to Children's Needs

Tailoring instructional strategies to meet the needs of children as individuals and as part of a group is essential for effective teaching.

- **Individual Learning**: Provide opportunities for one-on-one interactions, where teachers can offer personalized support and attention to each child's unique learning needs. These methods can be particularly effective for children who need additional help or are challenged.

- **Paired Learning**: Encourage paired learning activities, where children work in pairs to support each other's learning. These methods foster peer interaction, collaboration, and social skills development.

- **Small Group Instruction**: Use small group settings to focus on specific skills or concepts. Small groups allow for more targeted instruction and enable teachers to closely monitor and support individual progress.

- **Whole Group Activities**: Whole group instruction can be used for introducing new concepts, storytelling, and group discussions. This format helps build community and allows for shared learning experiences.

- **Learning Centers and Projects**: Incorporate learning centers and project-based learning to allow children to explore topics in depth and at their own pace. These configurations promote independent learning, critical thinking, and creativity.

Quick Tip

To structure your classroom environment effectively, remember the three C's: **Create** designated learning centers, **consistently** follow schedules and routines, and **customize** learning configurations to meet individual and group needs. This will help ensure a supportive and dynamic learning space for all children.

Applying a Flexible, Research-Based Repertoire of Teaching and Learning Approaches

Effectively promoting the diverse developmental needs of children requires a flexible and research-based approach to teaching and learning. This includes strategies that encourage critical-thinking skills, scaffold and differentiate instruction, support learning through technology, and integrate the curriculum.

1. Strategies to Encourage Critical-Thinking Skills and Inquiry

- **Questioning Techniques**: Use open-ended questions that prompt students to think deeply and explore different possibilities. Questions like "What do you think will happen if...?" or "Why do you think this is important?" stimulate critical thinking.

- **Problem-Based Learning (PBL)**: Engage students in real-world problems that require them to research, analyze, and propose solutions. PBL encourages inquiry and critical thinking as students work through complex issues.

- **Encouraging Exploration and Experimentation**: Provide opportunities for hands-on learning where students can experiment and explore concepts. Activities like science experiments, building projects, and exploratory play promote inquiry and critical thinking.

2. Scaffolding and Differentiation

- **Gradual Release of Responsibility**: Implement the "I do, we do, you do" model to scaffold learning. Start with direct instruction (I do), then engage students in guided practice (we do), and finally allow them to practice independently (you do).

- **Tailoring Instruction to Individual Needs**: Differentiate instruction by providing varied levels of support based on individual student needs. Use flexible grouping, provide choice in assignments, and offer additional resources for advanced learners or extra support for those who need it.

- **Using Formative Assessments**: Regularly assess students' understanding through formative assessments and adjust instruction accordingly. This allows for timely intervention and support.

3. Supporting Learning Through the Appropriate Use of Technology

- **Interactive Tools and Resources**: Use interactive whiteboards, educational apps, and online resources to enhance learning. These tools can make lessons more engaging and accessible.

- **Digital Literacy**: Teach students how to use technology responsibly and effectively. This includes basic computer skills, internet safety, and using technology for research and collaboration.

- **Blended Learning**: Combine traditional teaching methods with online learning. Blended learning allows students to work at their own pace and provides opportunities for personalized learning.

4. Using an Integrated Approach to Curriculum

- **Thematic Units**: Develop thematic units integrating multiple subject areas around a central theme. This approach helps students make connections between different subjects and see the relevance of what they are learning.

- **Project-Based Learning**: Implement projects requiring students to apply various disciplines' skills and knowledge. Projects can be designed to address real-world issues and promote deeper understanding.

- **Cross-Curricular Connections**: Identify and emphasize connections between subjects. For example, a lesson on the water cycle in science can be integrated with a reading assignment on weather in language arts.

Designing a Classroom to Accommodate Students with Physical and Emotional Disabilities

Creating an inclusive classroom environment that accommodates students with physical and emotional disabilities involves careful planning and thoughtful design. This ensures that all students have equitable access to learning opportunities and can participate fully in classroom activities.

The Least Restrictive Environment (LRE) is an educational setting that provides students with disabilities the opportunity to learn alongside their non-disabled peers to the greatest extent appropriate. It emphasizes inclusion in regular classroom activities while providing necessary supports and services. The goal is to ensure that students with disabilities receive an equitable education in an environment that fosters social, emotional, and academic growth.

1. Placement of Vision- and Hearing-Impaired Students

- **Vision-Impaired Students**:
  - **Seating**: Place vision-impaired students close to the front of the classroom where they have an unobstructed view of the teacher and instructional materials.
  - **Lighting**: Ensure the classroom has adequate lighting to help vision-impaired students see better. Use blinds or curtains to control glare.
  - **Materials**: Provide large print or Braille materials, and use tactile graphics and manipulatives to support learning.

- **Hearing-Impaired Students**:
    - **Seating**: Position hearing-impaired students where they can easily see the teacher's face and any visual aids. Preferably, seating should be away from sources of background noise.
    - **Sound Systems**: Use assistive listening devices such as frequency modulation (FM) systems to help students hear the teacher more clearly.
    - **Visual Aids**: Incorporate visual aids such as written instructions, captions for videos, and sign language interpreters if needed.

2. Space and Paths for Wheelchairs

- **Accessibility**: Ensure the classroom layout provides wide, clear paths for wheelchair mobility. Desks and tables should be at an appropriate height to accommodate wheelchair users.
- **Adaptable Furniture**: Use adjustable furniture that can be modified to meet the needs of students with varying physical abilities.
- **Accessible Storage**: Place frequently used materials and supplies at accessible heights for students in wheelchairs.

3. Accommodating Children with Challenging Behaviors

- **Behavioral Support Plans**: Develop individualized behavior intervention plans (BIPs) for students with challenging behaviors, outlining specific strategies and supports.
- **Calm Down Area**: Create a designated calm down area where students can go to regulate their emotions when they feel overwhelmed.
- **Consistent Routines**: Establish clear and consistent routines to provide a sense of stability and predictability for students with challenging behaviors.

4. Functional Behavior Assessment (FBA) Guidelines

- **Identify Problem Behaviors**: Clearly define and describe the challenging behaviors that need to be addressed.
- **Gather Information**: Collect data through observations, interviews, and behavior rating scales to understand the context and triggers of the behaviors.
- **Analyze Data**: Determine the function of the behavior (e.g., seeking attention, avoiding tasks) by analyzing the collected data.
- **Develop Intervention Plan**: Create an intervention plan that includes strategies for addressing the behavior, teaching alternative skills, and modifying the environment to support positive behavior.
- **Monitor and Adjust**: Continuously monitor the effectiveness of the intervention and make adjustments as needed to ensure success.

Adapting Technology for Students with Special Needs

Technology can be a powerful tool to support the learning and participation of students with special needs. Here are some adaptations for physical, emotional, and educational needs:

1. Adaptations for Physical Needs

- **Assistive Technology Devices**: Use devices such as adaptive keyboards, mouse alternatives (e.g., trackballs, joysticks), and touchscreens to accommodate students with physical disabilities.
- **Speech-to-Text Software**: Implement speech-to-text programs for students who have difficulty with writing or typing.
- **Augmentative and Alternative Communication (AAC)**: Provide AAC devices for students with speech impairments to help them communicate effectively.

2. Adaptations for Emotional Needs

- **Calming Apps**: Utilize apps that offer relaxation exercises, mindfulness activities, and calming music to help students manage anxiety and stress.
- **Social Skills Programs**: Implement software programs that teach and reinforce social skills through interactive activities and role-playing scenarios.
- **Behavior Tracking Tools**: Use digital tools to track and monitor behavior, providing immediate feedback and reinforcement for positive behaviors.

3. Adaptations for Educational Needs

- **Customized Learning Platforms**: Use educational software that allows for individualized learning paths, providing content at varying levels of difficulty to meet each student's needs.
- **Interactive Whiteboards**: Employ interactive whiteboards to engage students with interactive lessons that can be adapted for different learning styles.
- **Digital Textbooks and Resources**: Provide digital textbooks with features like text-to-speech, adjustable font sizes, and interactive content to support diverse learners.

By thoughtfully designing the classroom environment and leveraging adaptive technology, educators can create inclusive and supportive learning spaces that meet the diverse needs of all students.

Quick Tip

To ensure the least restrictive environment for students with physical and emotional disabilities, integrate adaptive seating and clear pathways for mobility, use assistive technologies for vision and hearing impairments, establish calm-down areas for emotional regulation, and implement behavior intervention plans. This promotes inclusivity while allowing students to participate fully in classroom activities.

Developmentally Appropriate Practices

This page intentionally left blank.

Developmentally Appropriate Practices – Practice Questions

1. Ms. Taylor is preparing her classroom for a new school year. She wants to create an environment that supports the diverse learning needs of her students, including those who require additional support and those who need more challenging activities. She decides to organize her classroom into various learning centers and establish consistent schedules and routines. Which of the following strategies best demonstrates her understanding of developmentally appropriate practices?

   A. Arrange the furniture to create large open spaces for group activities, place all learning materials in a central location, and allow children to choose activities freely throughout the day.

   B. Set up specific learning centers with distinct areas for reading, math, art, and science, provide labeled bins with accessible materials, and use a visual schedule to outline the day's activities.

   C. Group desks together to facilitate peer interaction, rotate the learning centers daily to prevent boredom, and implement flexible routines that change frequently to keep students engaged.

   D. Create individual workstations for each child, schedule frequent whole-group instruction sessions, and allow students to follow their own schedules based on personal preferences.

2. Mr. Rodriguez has noticed that some of his students struggle with transitions between activities and have difficulty focusing during large group instruction. To address this, he implements more structured routines and incorporates different learning configurations. Which of the following plans will most likely improve the classroom environment and support all students' learning needs?

   A. Implement a strict routine with exact times for each activity, use a visual schedule for the whole class, create paired learning opportunities during free play, and conduct most instruction in small groups.

   B. Allow students to choose their own activities throughout the day, use whole-group instruction for key lessons, implement a flexible schedule that changes weekly, and provide one-on-one support as needed.

   C. Establish a predictable daily schedule with a balance of whole-group, small-group, and individual activities, use visual and auditory cues for transitions, and set up centers that cater to different learning styles and developmental stages.

   D. Create a rotating schedule where students move between centers every 15 minutes, use large-group instruction for all core subjects, and provide individual feedback at the end of each day.

3. Ms. Rivera is planning a lesson on habitats for her third-grade class. She wants to encourage critical thinking and inquiry, scaffold learning, and integrate technology effectively. Which of the following plans best demonstrates her understanding of these concepts?

   A. Discuss what students already know about habitats, show a short video about different habitats, research an animal's habitat using their laptops, and create a presentation.

   B. Present a slideshow on different habitats, ask students to take notes, assign a worksheet with fill-in-the-blank questions about the slideshow, and have students discuss their answers in their cooperative groups.

   C. Provide a lecture on habitats, have students read a textbook chapter on the topic, and give a multiple-choice quiz to assess their understanding.

   D. Assign students to read an article on habitats at home, and then discuss their findings in class the next day.

4. Mr. Lee wants to implement an integrated approach to his third-grade curriculum by designing a project that involves science, language arts, and technology. He also wants to ensure that he differentiates and scaffolds instruction to meet the needs of all students. Which of the following projects best achieves these goals?

   A. Have students write a report on a scientific topic using the internet for research, then present their findings to the class using a digital presentation tool.

   B. Assign a science experiment to be done at home with parents, write a reflective journal entry about the experiment, and submit the journal online.

   C. Create a class blog where students post weekly summaries of their science lessons, comment on each other's posts, and discuss the content in groups.

   D. Organize a collaborative project where students research renewable energy, write a persuasive essay on its benefits, and create a multimedia presentation to advocate for their energy source.

5. Ms. Hernandez is designing a comprehensive learning environment for her early childhood classroom. She wants to include activities that support individual, cooperative, small-group, and whole-group learning, both indoors and outdoors. Which of the following plans best demonstrates her understanding of how to design these diverse learning environments?

   A. Indoor Individual Activity: Set up a quiet reading nook with a variety of books.
   Indoor Cooperative Activity: Create a building block center where children can work together to construct structures.
   Outdoor Small-Group Activity: Organize a nature scavenger hunt where small groups search for specific items.
   Outdoor Whole-Group Activity: Conduct a group storytelling session where children sit in a circle and listen to a story.

   B. Indoor Individual Activity: Provide a set of coloring books and crayons at each desk.
   Indoor Cooperative Activity: Have students work on a group art mural on the classroom wall.
   Outdoor Small-Group Activity: Set up individual drawing stations around the playground.
   Outdoor Whole-Group Activity: Lead a whole-class relay race in the schoolyard.

   C. Indoor Individual Activity: Assign worksheets for math practice at each child's desk.
   Indoor Cooperative Activity: Have children share toys during free play time.
   Outdoor Small-Group Activity: Plan a small group reading circle under a tree.
   Outdoor Whole-Group Activity: Organize a competitive sports tournament for the entire class.

   D. Indoor Individual Activity: Allow children to choose from a variety of puzzles and games at a designated center.
   Indoor Cooperative Activity: Facilitate a science experiment station where children can collaborate on simple experiments.
   Outdoor Small-Group Activity: Arrange a gardening project where small groups plant and care for flowers.
   Outdoor Whole-Group Activity: Conduct a class picnic where all students participate in games and activities together.

Number	Answer	Explanation
1.	B	**Correct Answer B:** Setting up learning centers demonstrates the creation of well-organized learning centers with accessible materials and a visual schedule, which are key components of developmentally appropriate practices. **Incorrect Answer A:** While large open spaces and allowing children to choose activities freely promote independence, having all materials in a central location can create confusion and limit the effectiveness of learning centers. **Incorrect Answer C:** Rotating learning centers daily can cause instability and disrupt students' ability to focus on specific areas. Flexible routines that change frequently can be confusing and counterproductive for young children. **Incorrect Answer D:** Individual workstations and frequent whole-group instruction do not cater to the diverse needs of all students and can limit opportunities for collaborative and hands-on learning.
2.	C	**Correct Answer C:** This method incorporates a balanced and predictable schedule, visual and auditory transition cues, and differentiated learning centers, which collectively address the diverse needs of students and improve focus and transitions. **Incorrect Answer A:** Implementing a strict routine and small group instruction—can be beneficial, but paired learning during free play and a rigid schedule may not address the needs of all students or allow for enough flexibility. **Incorrect Answer B:** Allowing students to choose activities and using a flexible schedule—can lead to inconsistency and lack of structure, which may not support students who struggle with transitions and focus. **Incorrect Answer D:** Rotating centers every 15 minutes can be disruptive and overwhelming. Also, relying solely on large-group instruction does not cater to individual learning needs or styles.
3.	A	**Correct Answer A:** This plan starts with activating prior knowledge (discussion), uses multimedia (short video) to engage students, incorporates technology for research (laptops), and encourages critical thinking and presentation skills (creating and sharing presentations). **Incorrect Answer B:** While the slideshow, taking notes, worksheet, and group discussion provides information and some engagement, it doesn't encourage critical thinking or use technology effectively. **Incorrect Answer C:** A lecture and textbook reading are more traditional methods and do not incorporate inquiry or technology. **Incorrect Answer D:** Assigning reading at home and discussing it lacks the integration of technology and doesn't scaffold learning effectively.

Developmentally Appropriate Practices

Number	Answer	Explanation
4.	D	**Correct Answer D:** This project integrates science (renewable energy research), language arts (writing a persuasive essay), and technology (creating a multimedia presentation). It also allows for differentiation and scaffolding by supporting collaboration and providing various entry points for different skill levels. **Incorrect Answer A:** While this method integrates research and presentation skills, it doesn't involve science experimentation or hands-on activities, and the differentiation is limited. **Incorrect Answer B:** This project involves science and language arts but lacks a significant technology component and doesn't provide opportunities for differentiation and scaffolding within the classroom. **Incorrect Answer C:** Creating a class blog incorporates technology and language arts but doesn't integrate science experimentation or ensure differentiation and scaffolding in a collaborative setting.
5.	D	**Correct Answer D:** This plan effectively incorporates individual activities (puzzles and games), cooperative activities (science experiments), small-group activities (gardening project), and whole-group activities (class picnic) in both indoor and outdoor settings, allowing children to play, explore, and discover in various contexts. **Incorrect Answer A:** While the indoor activities are appropriate, the outdoor whole-group activity (storytelling session) might not be as engaging for all students in a large group setting, and it misses the active play element. **Incorrect Answer B:** The outdoor small-group activity (individual drawing stations) does not involve group interaction, and the whole-group activity (relay race) might not cater to diverse interests and abilities. **Incorrect Answer C:** The indoor cooperative activity (sharing toys) and the outdoor whole-group activity (competitive sports tournament) may not provide structured opportunities for learning and collaboration and might not be inclusive for all children.

IV. Professionalism, Family, and Community

Understanding the interconnected roles of professionalism, family, and community is crucial in early childhood education. Educators must uphold high standards of professional conduct and demonstrate a commitment to continuous learning and ethical practices. Building strong, collaborative relationships with families supports children's development and education.

Effective communication and family partnerships ensure that educational experiences align with children's home environments and cultural backgrounds. Additionally, engaging with the broader community provides valuable resources and support systems, enriching the academic environment and fostering a sense of belonging and inclusion for children and their families. Educators create a holistic and supportive learning experience that nurtures the whole child by integrating professionalism, family, and community.

The following concepts are discussed in this content category:

- Ethical Standards and Professional Guidelines in Early Childhood Education
- Continuous, Collaborative Learning to Inform Practice
- Integrated Role of Other Professionals in Children's Care and Education
- Engaging and Supporting Families and Communities through Respectful, Reciprocal Relationships
- Involving Families and Communities in Young Children's Development and Learning

Ethical Standards and Professional Guidelines in Early Childhood Education

Early childhood educators must adhere to high ethical standards to ensure the well-being and development of the children they serve. Familiarity with the codes of ethical conduct established by professional organizations is essential.

We recommend reviewing the websites of these organizations. Memorizing content on these websites is not necessary, but becoming familiar with the information concerning the codes of ethics is.

Two organizations early childhood educators must become familiar with are:

- **The National Association for the Education of Young Children (NAEYC)** – This association provides a comprehensive code of ethics that guides educators in their professional conduct, emphasizing the importance of respect, confidentiality, and the promotion of positive development and learning experiences for all children.

- **The Division of Early Childhood (DEC)** – This association offers a code of ethics that focuses on the specific needs of children with disabilities and their families, advocating for inclusive practices and individualized support.

Individuals with Disabilities Education Act (IDEA)

The Individuals with Disabilities Education Act (IDEA) is a federal law that ensures children with disabilities receive a free and appropriate public education (FAPE). IDEA mandates that children with disabilities receive an Individualized Education Program (IEP) tailored to their unique needs. It also ensures that these children are educated in the least restrictive environment (LRE) possible, alongside their non-disabled peers to the greatest extent appropriate. IDEA outlines specific rights and protections for children with disabilities and their families, including procedural safeguards and the right to due process.

Quick Tip

When answering questions about accommodating students with disabilities, remember the importance of the least restrictive environment (LRE). LRE emphasizes educating students with disabilities alongside their non-disabled peers to the maximum extent appropriate. As these are often correct, look for answer choices highlighting inclusion, integration, and providing appropriate support within general education settings.

Section 504 of the Rehabilitation Act

Section 504 of the Rehabilitation Act protects the rights of individuals with disabilities in programs and activities that receive federal financial assistance, including public schools. Under Section 504, children with disabilities must have equal access to education and accommodations that allow them to participate fully in school activities. A 504 Plan outlines the specific accommodations, modifications, and services the child needs to effectively access the curriculum and school environment.

Family Educational Rights and Privacy Act (FERPA)

The Family Educational Rights and Privacy Act (FERPA) is a federal law protecting student privacy, specifically concerning student information and records. FERPA grants parents and eligible students (those over 18 years old) the right to access and review the student's education records, request amendments to inaccurate or misleading information, and consent to disclose personally identifiable information from the records, except under certain permitted circumstances. Educators must understand and comply with FERPA requirements to ensure confidentiality and proper handling of student information.

Quick Tip

To remember who has the right to access school records under FERPA, think **"P.A.S.T."**:

- **Parents**: They have full rights to their child's educational records until the child turns 18 or attends a school beyond the high school level.

- **Authorized School Officials**: They can access records for legitimate educational interests.

- **Students**: Once they turn 18 or attend a postsecondary institution, they control access to their records. Parents no longer have this right unless the student authorizes it.

- **Third Parties**: Only with written consent from parents or eligible students, except in specific situations like court orders or health and safety emergencies, can third parties access student records..

Health Insurance Portability and Accountability Act (HIPAA)

The Health Insurance Portability and Accountability Act (HIPAA) is a federal law that sets standards for protecting health information. While HIPAA primarily applies to healthcare providers, it also impacts schools that provide health services to students. Schools must ensure that students' health information is protected and disclosed only following HIPAA regulations. This includes maintaining the confidentiality of health records and ensuring that information sharing is done securely and for legitimate purposes.

Continuous, Collaborative Learning to Inform Practice

In early childhood education, continuous, collaborative learning is essential for enhancing instructional practices and improving student outcomes. This approach involves educators engaging in ongoing professional development, sharing insights, and working together to analyze and refine their teaching strategies.

Importance of Continuous Professional Growth

Continuous professional growth is essential for early childhood educators to keep up with the latest research, educational practices, and technological advancements. By seeking opportunities for professional development, educators can improve their teaching strategies, enhance their understanding of child development, and ultimately provide higher-quality education to their students. Opportunities for professional growth can include attending workshops, enrolling in courses, obtaining advanced degrees, and participating in professional organizations.

Collaborative Learning Communities

Collaborative learning communities play a crucial role in the professional development of early childhood educators. These communities can be formed within schools (on-site), extend to homes, or occur at conferences and through data teams. Engaging in collaborative learning allows educators to share knowledge, discuss challenges, and develop new strategies together. It fosters a sense of support and collective responsibility for improving educational practices. Essential skills for participating in collaborative learning communities include effective communication, active listening, teamwork, and giving and receiving constructive feedback.

- **On-Site**: School-based professional learning communities (PLCs) where teachers meet regularly to discuss student progress, share teaching strategies, and analyze data.
- **Homes**: Engaging with parents and caregivers through home visits or community meetings to gain insights into children's backgrounds and needs.
- **Conferences**: Attending educational conferences to network with other professionals, learn about new research, and participate in workshops.
- **Data Teams**: Collaborating with colleagues to analyze student data, identify trends, and develop action plans for improvement.

Importance of Reflection to Inform Practice

Reflection is a critical component of professional growth and improvement. It involves analyzing one's teaching practices, evaluating their effectiveness, and identifying areas for improvement. Regular reflection allows educators to adapt their methods to meet the needs of their students. Reflective practices include keeping a teaching journal, seeking feedback from peers and supervisors, and self-assessment through video recordings of teaching sessions. Educators can make informed decisions about modifying and enhancing their instructional techniques by engaging in reflection.

Quick Tip

Self-reflection for teachers and students is an effective practice. In fact, it is often found in the correct answer choices on the exam. Therefore, slow down if you see the term self-reflection or a phrase like it because it could be the correct answer.

Classroom Scenario: Kindergarten PLCs Analyzing Data and Improving Instruction

At Maplewood Elementary School, the kindergarten team of teachers meets every Wednesday afternoon for their Professional Learning Community (PLC) session. The team consists of five kindergarten teachers, a reading specialist, and the school's instructional coach.

Objective: The primary goal of this week's PLC meeting is to analyze recent reading assessment data and develop strategies to improve literacy instruction for all students.

Scenario:

1. **Data Review:** The meeting begins with the instructional coach distributing copies of the latest reading assessment data, which includes scores from both formative assessments (such as running records and sight word recognition tests) and summative assessments (like standardized reading tests). The data is broken down by class as well as by individual student performance.

2. **Identifying Trends:** The teachers spend the first part of the meeting reviewing the data. They use color-coded charts to identify trends and patterns. For example, they notice that many students are struggling with phonemic awareness and decoding skills. They also observe that some students are not making expected progress in comprehension despite performing well in other areas.

3. **Collaborative Discussion:** The instructional coach facilitates a discussion where each teacher shares insights and observations from their classroom experiences. Ms. Johnson mentions that her

students respond well to hands-on phonics activities, while Mr. Lee notes that his students enjoy interactive read-alouds that emphasize story structure and vocabulary.

4. **Setting Goals:** Based on the data analysis and discussion, the team sets specific, measurable goals for the next month. For example, they agree to focus on improving phonemic awareness by incorporating daily phonics games and activities. They also decide to implement more comprehension strategies, such as think-alouds and story mapping, during read-aloud sessions.

5. **Developing Action Plans:** The teachers collaboratively develop action plans for their classrooms. Each teacher selects two or three new instructional strategies to implement over the next few weeks. They also plan to use formative assessments, such as exit tickets and quick checks, to monitor students' progress and adjust instruction as needed.

6. **Resource Sharing:** The reading specialist shares a list of recommended resources, including phonics games, story maps, and comprehension question stems. The teachers discuss how they can integrate these resources into their daily lessons and share ideas for differentiating instruction to meet the diverse needs of their students.

7. **Reflective Practice:** The meeting concludes with a reflection period. The teachers reflect on their previous instructional strategies and how the new approaches might address the identified areas of need. They commit to observing each other's classrooms over the next month to provide feedback and support.

8. **Follow-Up:** The instructional coach schedules a follow-up meeting in four weeks to review progress and make any necessary adjustments to the action plans. The teachers leave the meeting feeling empowered and equipped with new strategies to enhance their literacy instruction and support student learning.

By engaging in this collaborative PLC process, the kindergarten teachers at Maplewood Elementary School effectively use data to inform their instruction, share best practices, and continuously improve their teaching strategies to meet the needs of their students.

Multi-Tiered System of Supports (MTSS) in Early Education

The Multi-Tiered System of Supports (MTSS) is a comprehensive framework designed to provide targeted support to all students, ensuring that every child receives the appropriate level of instruction and intervention to meet their academic, behavioral, and social-emotional needs. In early education, MTSS is particularly effective in identifying and addressing learning difficulties and developmental delays at an early stage. The framework consists of three tiers:

- Tier 1 includes high-quality, evidence-based instruction and universal screening for all students.

- Tier 2 involves targeted interventions for students who need additional support beyond the core curriculum.

- Tier 3 provides intensive, individualized interventions for students with significant needs.

By implementing MTSS, early childhood educators can systematically monitor student progress, adjust instruction based on data, and ensure that every child receives the support necessary to succeed.

Quick Tip

When answering questions about MTSS, remember the following:

Tier 1 – All

Tier 2 – Some

Tier 3 – Few

MTSS in early childhood education emphasizes the importance of collaboration among educators, specialists, and families to create a cohesive support system for young learners. Teachers use data from universal screenings and ongoing assessments to identify students who may need additional help and then work with specialists, such as reading specialists, special educators, and school psychologists, to develop and implement targeted interventions.

Family involvement is also critical, as parents provide valuable insights into their child's needs and progress. Through regular communication and collaboration, educators and families can create individualized support plans that address each child's unique strengths and challenges. MTSS helps build a strong foundation for lifelong learning and development by fostering a proactive and inclusive approach to early education.

Integrated Role of Other Professionals in Children's Care and Education

Early childhood education benefits greatly from the collaboration of various professionals who contribute to children's holistic development and well-being. Understanding the roles and responsibilities of these professionals is crucial for educators to support their students effectively.

Special Educators

Special educators work with children who have diverse learning needs and disabilities. They develop Individualized Education Programs (IEPs) tailored to each child's unique requirements. Special educators provide specialized instruction, modify the curriculum, and implement strategies to help students succeed academically and socially. Collaboration with general education teachers ensures that students receive appropriate accommodations and modifications in the classroom.

Reading Specialists

Reading specialists focus on improving literacy skills among young learners. They assess reading levels, identify struggling readers, and implement targeted interventions to enhance reading proficiency. Reading specialists also support teachers by providing resources, strategies, and professional development opportunities to improve literacy instruction across the curriculum.

Speech and Hearing Specialists

Speech and hearing specialists, or speech-language pathologists (SLPs), assess and treat communication disorders in children. They work with students who have difficulties with speech, language, hearing, and related skills. SLPs create individualized therapy plans to address speech and language delays, articulation issues, and auditory processing disorders. Collaboration with classroom teachers ensures that speech and language goals are integrated into daily classroom activities.

Physical and Occupational Therapists

Physical therapists (PTs) and occupational therapists (OTs) support children with physical and motor development needs. PTs help children improve their gross motor skills, such as walking, running, and jumping, while OTs focus on fine motor skills, such as writing, cutting, and manipulating objects. These therapists develop individualized plans and work with children in classroom and specialized settings to enhance their physical abilities and independence.

Specialists in Gifted Education

Specialists in gifted education identify and support students who demonstrate advanced abilities and talents. They design enrichment programs and differentiated instruction to challenge gifted learners and help them reach their full potential. These specialists work closely with teachers to modify the curriculum, provide extension activities, and create opportunities for gifted students to explore their interests and develop their skills.

School Psychologists

School psychologists play a vital role in supporting students' mental health and emotional well-being. They conduct assessments to identify learning and behavioral issues, provide counseling services, and develop intervention plans. School psychologists collaborate with teachers, parents, and other professionals to create a supportive and inclusive learning environment. They offer strategies to manage classroom behavior, support social-emotional development, and address mental health concerns.

Quick Tip

When collaborating with other professionals in early childhood education, remember the importance of open communication and teamwork. Regularly share insights and updates with special educators, reading specialists, speech and hearing specialists, physical and occupational therapists, specialists in gifted education, and school psychologists. This collaborative approach ensures a comprehensive and supportive learning environment that meets the diverse needs of all students.

Communicating with Children, Families, and Peers

Technology enhances communication between educators, children, families, and peers. It can bridge gaps and foster a collaborative and inclusive educational environment when used appropriately. The following are a few ways in which technology can aid in communicating with children, families, and peers.

- **Teacher Websites** – Teacher websites provide a centralized platform for parents to access important information, announcements, and resources, enhancing communication between teachers and families. These websites can host educational resources, lesson plans, and activities that support student learning outside of classroom hours. Teacher websites can offer interactive content and activities that engage students in their learning process.

- **Hybrid Learning** – Hybrid learning combines in-person and online instruction, offering flexibility for students to learn at their own pace and on their own schedule. It allows students to access learning materials and participate in lessons from anywhere, accommodating different learning styles and needs. Hybrid learning can integrate a variety of digital tools and resources, enriching the educational experience and fostering independent learning skills.

- **Video Conferencing** - Video conferencing enables real-time interaction between teachers, students, and parents, fostering a sense of community and immediate feedback. It supports distance learning by allowing students to participate in live lessons and discussions from remote locations. Video conferencing tools facilitate collaboration on projects and group activities, promoting teamwork and communication skills.

- **Google Docs** - Google Docs allows multiple users to work on the same document simultaneously, promoting collaborative learning and peer feedback. Students and teachers can access and edit documents from any device with an internet connection, ensuring that learning materials are always available. Teachers can provide real-time feedback and comments on student work, enhancing the revision and learning process.

- **Google Classroom** - Google Classroom helps teachers organize assignments, materials, and grades in one place, simplifying classroom management. It provides a platform for teachers to communicate with students and parents, share announcements, and answer questions. Google Classroom integrates seamlessly with other Google tools, such as Google Docs and Google Drive, streamlining the workflow and enhancing productivity.

- **Digital Portfolios** – Digital portfolios are an effective way to document and share a child's progress and achievements. These portfolios can include photos, videos, scanned artwork, and other digital artifacts that showcase a child's development over time. They allow parents to see their child's work and progress in real time, fostering greater involvement in their child's education. Additionally, digital portfolios can be easily shared with other educators and specialists, facilitating collaboration and continuous support.

- **Online Report Cards** – Online report cards streamline reporting student progress to families. They provide a convenient and accessible way for parents to receive updates on their child's academic performance, attendance, and behavior. Online report cards can include detailed comments from teachers and graphs and charts that illustrate the child's progress over time. This technology ensures timely communication and helps parents stay informed and engaged in their child's education.

- **Embedded Instruction** – Embedded instruction integrates technology into daily classroom activities and lessons. This approach can include interactive whiteboards, educational apps, and online resources that enhance learning experiences. For example, teachers can use interactive storytelling apps to support literacy development or math games to reinforce numerical skills. Embedded instruction makes learning more engaging and accessible, catering to diverse learning styles and needs.

Quick Tip

Technology can greatly enhance the classroom experience by providing diverse resources and interactive learning opportunities. However, it cannot replace the critical role of a highly effective teacher who brings expertise, empathy, and personalized guidance to foster student growth and engagement. Always balance the use of technology with meaningful teacher-student interactions to maximize learning outcomes.

Professional Resource and Collaboration

Technology also serves as a valuable professional resource for educators, enabling them to access information, collaborate with peers, and engage in ongoing professional development.

- **Professional Learning Networks (PLNs)** – Educators can join online communities and professional learning networks (PLNs) to connect with peers, share resources, and discuss best practices. Platforms such as Twitter, LinkedIn, and specialized forums provide opportunities for educators to stay updated on the latest research, trends, and innovations in early childhood education. PLNs foster a culture of continuous learning and professional growth.

- **Webinars and Online Courses** – Webinars and online courses offer flexible and convenient professional development opportunities. Educators can participate in training sessions, workshops, and courses from their homes or classrooms. These resources cover various topics, from classroom management strategies to integrating technology into the curriculum. Educators can enhance their skills and knowledge by engaging in online professional development, ultimately benefiting their students.

- **Collaborative Tools** – Collaborative tools such as Google Docs, Microsoft Teams, and other cloud-based platforms enable educators to collaborate on projects, share lesson plans, and communicate effectively. These tools support real-time collaboration and ensure all team members can access the latest information and resources. Educators can create a more cohesive and supportive teaching environment by leveraging collaborative technology.

Engaging and Supporting Families and Communities through Respectful, Reciprocal Relationships

Building strong, respectful relationships with families and communities is essential for the success and well-being of children in early childhood education. Effective engagement and support strategies help create a collaborative environment where families feel valued and connected to their children's learning journey.

Building Positive Relationships with Families and Communities

- **Welcoming Environment** – Creating a welcoming environment in the classroom and school is the first step in building positive relationships with families and communities. This includes displaying student work, providing comfortable spaces for parents to visit, and being approachable and available for conversations. A welcoming environment fosters trust and encourages families to be more involved in their child's education.

- **Family Involvement Activities** – Organizing family involvement activities, such as family nights, open houses, and cultural events, provides opportunities for families to engage with the school community. These events allow families to connect with teachers, other families, and the broader community, strengthening their sense of belonging and partnership.

- **Respect for Diversity** – Recognizing and respecting families' diverse backgrounds, cultures, and values is crucial. Educators should strive to understand and celebrate this diversity by incorporating culturally relevant materials and practices into the classroom. This approach helps families feel respected and acknowledged, fostering positive relationships.

Communication Strategies and Tools to Foster Relationships with Families

- **Informal Conversations** – Regular informal conversations with families help build rapport and trust. These can occur during drop-off and pick-up times, school events, or casual interactions. Informal conversations provide a relaxed setting for sharing information and addressing family concerns.

- **Parent-Teacher Conferences** – Scheduled parent-teacher conferences are a more formal way to discuss a child's progress, strengths, and areas for improvement. Conferences should be conducted with respect and empathy, focusing on the child's development and how families and teachers can work together to support their growth.

- **Technology Integration** – Using technology to communicate with families can enhance engagement and provide convenient ways for families to stay informed. Email, classroom apps, and school websites can be used to share updates, resources, and important information. Additionally, virtual meetings and video calls offer flexible options for families who cannot attend in-person meetings.

Connecting Families to Needed Resources

- **Resource Identification** – Educators should be knowledgeable about community resources that can support families in various aspects of their lives. This includes mental health services, health care providers, adult education programs, English-language instruction, and economic assistance programs.

- **Referral Process** – Developing a clear and respectful referral process is essential for connecting families to the necessary resources. This involves understanding the family's needs, providing them with information about available services, and guiding them through accessing these resources.

- **Partnerships with Community Organizations** – Building partnerships with local community organizations can enhance the support network available to families. Schools can collaborate with these organizations to provide workshops, informational sessions, and direct services to families, creating a comprehensive support system.

Involving Families and Communities in Young Children's Development and Learning

Engaging families and communities in the educational process is crucial for the holistic development of young children. Involving families in curriculum, assessment, and transitions enhances the learning experience and ensures that children receive consistent support at home and school.

Strategies to Engage Families in Their Child's Curriculum and Assessment of Learning

- **Curriculum Nights and Workshops** – Hosting curriculum nights and workshops for families helps them understand the educational goals and methods used in the classroom. These events can provide hands-on experiences with the curriculum, allowing families to see what their children are learning and how they can support this learning at home.

- **Family Learning Activities** – Incorporating family learning activities that can be completed at home strengthens the connection between school and home. These activities might include reading together, completing simple science experiments, or engaging in math games. Providing families with materials and guidance on supporting their child's learning reinforces classroom concepts and fosters a collaborative approach to education.

- **Regular Communication and Feedback** – It is essential to maintain regular communication with families about their child's progress. This can be done through newsletters, progress reports, and parent-teacher conferences. Encouraging families to provide feedback and share their observations helps create a two-way dialogue, ensuring that the child's learning needs are fully understood and addressed.

Collaborating with Families and Colleagues to Make Informed Decisions

- **Collaborative Decision-Making Protocols** – Establishing protocols for collaborative decision-making ensures that families and educators work together to support the child's education. This might include regular meetings with parents, teachers, and specialists to discuss the child's progress and make joint decisions regarding instructional strategies, interventions, and supports.

- **Multi-Disciplinary Teams** – Forming multi-disciplinary teams that include other content area teachers, special educators, school psychologists, and other specialists can provide comprehensive support for the child. These teams work collaboratively with families to develop and implement individualized education plans (IEPs) and other tailored supports.

- **Shared Goals and Action Plans** – Creating shared goals and action plans with input from both families and educators ensures that everyone is working towards the same objectives. Documenting these goals and regularly reviewing progress helps keep everyone aligned and focused on the child's development.

Strategies to Address Transitions Within and Among Programs

- **Transition Plans** – Developing detailed transition plans helps children move smoothly between different educational settings, such as from preschool to kindergarten or from one grade to the next. Transition plans should include strategies for familiarizing the child with the new environment, routines, and expectations.

- **Orientation Sessions** – Hosting orientation sessions for children and families prior to a transition can alleviate anxiety and build confidence. These sessions might include tours of the new classroom, meetings with future teachers, and opportunities for children to engage in activities in the new setting.

- **Continuous Communication** – Maintaining continuous communication with families during transitions is vital. This includes providing updates on the child's adjustment, sharing resources to support the transition at home, and being available to address any concerns or questions families might have.

- **Peer Support Programs** – Implementing peer support programs, such as buddy systems, can help children feel more comfortable during transitions. Pairing a child with a peer who is already familiar with the new environment can provide social support and a sense of belonging.

Classroom Scenario: Multi-Disciplinary Teams Supporting Students

Setting: Oakwood Elementary School, Kindergarten Classroom

Objective: Provide comprehensive support for a student, Timmy, through a multi-disciplinary team to address his academic and developmental needs.

Background: Timmy is a kindergartener who exhibits difficulties in speech articulation, fine motor skills, and social interactions. He has already gone through the MTSS process and is being referred to special education. His teacher, Ms. Miller, wants to be sure she is collaborating with a multidisciplinary team to support Timmy.

Scenario:

1. **Initial Observation and Referral:** Ms. Miller notices that Timmy struggles with clear speech, has difficulty holding a pencil properly, and often isolates himself from group activities. She decides to participate in the multi-disciplinary team to support Timmy's success.

2. **The Multi-Disciplinary Team:** Ms. Miller joins the school's special education coordinator, Ms. Johnson, to discuss Timmy's needs. The multi-disciplinary team includes:

   - Ms. Miller (Classroom Teacher)

   - Ms. Johnson (Special Education Coordinator)

   - Ms. Smith (Speech-Language Pathologist)

- Mr. Carter (Occupational Therapist)

- Ms. Brown (School Psychologist)

- Timmy's parents, Mr. and Mrs. Wilson

3. **Collaborative Team Meeting:** The team schedules a meeting to discuss Timmy's needs and develop a plan of action. During the meeting, each member provides insights based on their observations and expertise:

   - **Ms. Miller:** Shares classroom observations and concerns about Timmy's speech, fine motor skills, and social interactions.

   - **Ms. Smith:** Conducts a preliminary speech and language assessment and discusses potential speech therapy goals.

   - **Mr. Carter:** Evaluates Timmy's fine motor skills and suggests activities to improve his pencil grip and hand strength.

   - **Ms. Brown:** Assesses Timmy's social interactions and emotional well-being, offering strategies to support his social development.

   - **Mr. and Mrs. Wilson:** Share insights about Timmy's behavior and development at home, expressing their concerns and hopes for his progress.

4. **Developing an Individualized Education Plan (IEP):** Based on the discussion, the team collaboratively develops an IEP tailored to Timmy's needs. The IEP includes:

   - **Speech Therapy:** Weekly sessions with Ms. Smith to improve articulation and communication skills.

   - **Occupational Therapy:** Bi-weekly sessions with Mr. Carter to enhance fine motor skills and provide adaptive tools for writing.

   - **Social Skills Support:** Small group sessions with Ms. Brown to help Timmy build social interactions and peer relationships.

   - **Classroom Accommodations:** Ms. Miller implements specific strategies in the classroom, such as using visual aids for speech practice and integrating fine motor activities into daily routines.

5. **Implementing the IEP:** The team ensures that the IEP is implemented consistently. Ms. Miller integrates the suggested accommodations and collaborates with the specialists to monitor Timmy's progress. Regular check-ins and updates are scheduled to review Timmy's development and make necessary adjustments to the IEP.

6. **Ongoing Collaboration:** The multi-disciplinary team continues to work closely with Timmy's parents, providing updates and involving them in decision-making. They also maintain open communication with each other, sharing observations and progress reports to ensure a coordinated approach to Timmy's support.

Outcome: With the comprehensive support provided by the multi-disciplinary team, Timmy begins to show improvement in his speech, fine motor skills, and social interactions. The collaborative efforts of the team, combined with regular communication and tailored interventions, create a supportive environment that fosters Timmy's development and success.

By leveraging the expertise of various professionals and maintaining a strong partnership with Timmy's family, the multi-disciplinary team at Oakwood Elementary School demonstrates the effectiveness of a collaborative approach in supporting the diverse needs of young learners.

Professionalism, Family, and Community – Practice Questions

1. Ms. Davis is an early childhood teacher who is reviewing one of her student's Individualized Education Program (IEP). Which of the following practices aligns with the general principles of the Individuals with Disabilities Education Act (IDEA) and ensures she follows the student's IEP?

   A. Place the student in a separate classroom for all activities to ensure specialized instruction.

   B. Include the student in the general education classroom with appropriate supports and services.

   C. Provide the student with a modified curriculum even if it differs significantly from their peers' curriculum.

   D. Limiting the student's participation in school activities to ensure the student's and peers' safety.

2. Which of the following scenarios best exemplifies compliance with Section 504 of the Rehabilitation Act in a preschool setting?

   A. A preschool only accepts students who do not require any special accommodations.

   B. A preschool encourages parents of children with disabilities to hire private aides for classroom support.

   C. A preschool provides accommodations only if they do not require significant changes to the classroom environment.

   D. A preschool develops individualized plans to provide necessary accommodations for students with disabilities.

3. Which practice would **NOT** comply with the Family Educational Rights and Privacy Act (FERPA)?

   A. Allow parents to review and request amendments to their child's educational records.

   B. Post students' grades publicly on a classroom bulletin board without identifying information attached.

   C. Share a student's educational records with a school volunteer to help with tutoring sessions.

   D. Discuss a student's academic performance with another teacher during a professional meeting.

4. What is one of the key benefits of engaging in professional learning communities (PLCs) for early childhood educators?

   A. To provide a platform for teachers to share insights and develop new strategies.

   B. To ensure that all teachers follow the same teaching methods

   C. To reduce the need for individualized professional development.

   D. To allow teachers to compete for the best student performance outcomes.

5. During a PLC meeting, the kindergarten teachers at Maplewood Elementary School reviewed reading assessment data and noticed many students struggle with phonemic awareness. What would be the most effective strategy for this group of teachers to use?

   A. Implement daily activities that focus on identifying and manipulating sounds in words, use formative assessments to monitor progress, and discuss findings at the next PLC.

   B. Increase the time spent on silent reading daily, record how many words students read, and analyze that data at the next PLC.

   C. Assign additional homework focused on phonics skills, grade the homework, and discuss the grades with parents and members of the PLC.

   D. Reduce the number of PLC meetings so teachers can focus on student learning rather than being in meetings with colleagues.

6. Ms. Green is a kindergarten teacher who notices that one of her students, Lily, struggles with both fine motor skills and speech articulation. Which of the following steps should Ms. Green take to provide the most comprehensive support for Lily?

    A. Refer Lily to the school's reading specialist for additional literacy support.

    B. Request a meeting with the school psychologist to discuss behavioral interventions.

    C. Design a classroom-based intervention plan before consulting other professionals to see if that helps.

    D. Collaborate with a physical therapist and a speech-language pathologist to develop an integrated support plan.

7. Which of the following best describes the primary goal of implementing a Multi-Tiered System of Supports (MTSS) in early education?

    A. To provide high-quality, evidence-based instruction to all students and systematically identify those who need additional support.

    B. To enhance traditional classroom instruction with specialized, one-on-one tutoring for students who need support.

    C. To focus on the academic needs of students, setting aside behavioral and social-emotional aspects.

    D. To delay interventions until students reach higher grade levels to assess their long-term needs better.

8. Ms. Rodriguez is planning the transition for her preschool students to kindergarten. Which of the following strategies would best support a smooth transition?

    A. Sending home a list of kindergarten expectations for parents to review with their children.

    B. Hosting a meeting with kindergarten teachers to discuss the curriculum.

    C. Developing a detailed transition plan that includes visits to the kindergarten classroom, meeting future teachers, and practicing new routines.

    D. Giving the children extra homework to prepare them for the increased academic demands of kindergarten.

9. Ms. Lee is an early childhood teacher who notices that one of her students, Michael, has difficulty focusing and participating in class activities. She learns that Michael's family is going through a divorce. What can Ms. Lee do to support Michael?

    A. Set aside time to talk to Michael about the divorce.

    B. Recommend Michael see the school psychologist.

    C. Provide emotional support and a stable classroom environment.

    D. Maintain a consistent homework schedule.

10. How can a teacher use self-assessment techniques to reflect on teaching practices and the learning environment? Choose **ALL** that apply.

    ☐ A. Keep a reflective journal to document daily teaching experiences and student interactions.

    ☐ B. Seek feedback from colleagues through peer observations and discussions.

    ☐ C. Review and analyze student performance data to identify areas for instructional improvement.

    ☐ D. Send behavioral data home to parents and reflect on classroom procedures and expectations.

    ☐ E. Attend professional development workshops and apply new strategies in the classroom.

Number	Answer	Explanation
1.	B	**Correct Answer B**: This answer reflects the IDEA principle of educating children in the least restrictive environment (LRE). **Incorrect Answer A**: Placing the student in a separate classroom is the opposite of the LRE principle of IDEA. **Incorrect Answer C**: While modifications can be necessary, this does not fully reflect the inclusive approach of IDEA. **Incorrect Answer D**: This does not support the goal of full inclusion under IDEA.
2.	D	**Correct Answer D**: Developing individualized plans to provide necessary accommodations for students with disabilities aligns with the requirements of Section 504 to ensure equal access and opportunity. **Incorrect Answer A**: A preschool only accepts students who do not require any special accommodations. This violates Section 504, which mandates accommodations for students with disabilities. **Incorrect Answer B**: Encouraging parents of children with disabilities to hire private aides for classroom support shifts the responsibility away from the school, contrary to Section 504. **Incorrect Answer C**: Providing accommodations only if they do not require significant changes to the classroom environment goes against Section 504. Section 504 requires necessary accommodations regardless of the extent of changes needed.
3.	C	**Correct Answer C**: This practice is not in compliance with FERPA as it involves sharing confidential educational records with individuals who are not authorized to access this information without proper consent. **Incorrect Answer A**: This practice follows FERPA, which grants parents the right to access and request changes to their child's educational records. **Incorrect Answer B**: Generally, FERPA does not allow public posting of grades; however, this choice specifies that no identifying information is attached, which can comply with FERPA under certain circumstances. **Incorrect Answer D**: This is typically acceptable under FERPA as long as the discussion is relevant to the student's educational interests and occurs in a professional context.

Number	Answer	Explanation
4.	A	**Correct Answer A**: PLCs foster a collaborative environment where teachers can learn from each other, discuss challenges, and develop effective instructional strategies together. **Incorrect Answer B**: PLCs encourage collaboration and sharing of best practices but do not mandate identical teaching methods for all teachers. **Incorrect Answer C**: While PLCs are valuable, they complement rather than replace individualized professional development opportunities. **Incorrect Answer D**: PLCs focus on collaboration and collective improvement, not competition among teachers.
5.	A	**Correct Answer A**: This strategy directly targets phonemic awareness, involves regular monitoring of student progress, and leverages the collaborative nature of PLCs for continuous improvement. **Incorrect Answer B**: While silent reading is beneficial, it does not specifically address phonemic awareness, which focuses on the ability to hear and manipulate sounds. **Incorrect Answer C**: Although phonics is important, this approach does not directly address phonemic awareness, and it also focuses on homework rather than classwork. **Incorrect Answer D**: This option undermines the collaborative and reflective nature of PLCs, which are crucial for analyzing data and developing effective instructional strategies.
6.	D	**Correct Answer D**: This approach ensures that Lily receives targeted support for both her fine motor skills and speech articulation from specialized professionals, providing a comprehensive and effective intervention. **Incorrect Answer A**: While literacy support is important, it does not address Lily's specific needs related to fine motor skills and speech articulation. **Incorrect Answer B**: Although involving the school psychologist can be helpful, it does not directly address Lily's fine motor and speech articulation challenges. **Incorrect Answer C**: While classroom interventions are beneficial, they may not be sufficient to address Lily's specific needs without the expertise of specialized professionals.
7.	A	**Correct Answer A**: MTSS aims to ensure that all students receive appropriate instruction and interventions tailored to their individual needs based on data and continuous monitoring. **Incorrect Answer B**: While MTSS includes targeted interventions, it does not replace traditional instruction but supplements it as needed. **Incorrect Answer C**: MTSS addresses the whole child, including academic, behavioral, and social-emotional needs, rather than focusing solely on academics. **Incorrect Answer D**: MTSS emphasizes early identification and intervention to address issues as soon as they are identified rather than waiting until later grades.

Number	Answer	Explanation
8.	C	**Correct Answer C**: This comprehensive approach helps familiarize children with their new environment and expectations, easing anxiety and building confidence. **Incorrect Answer A**: While informative, this approach lacks the hands-on, experiential learning that helps children adapt to new settings. **Incorrect Answer B**: While collaboration among teachers is important, this strategy does not directly involve or benefit the children transitioning. **Incorrect Answer D**: This approach may increase stress rather than support a smooth transition, as it focuses on academic preparation rather than familiarizing children with the new environment and routines.
9.	C	**Correct Answer C**: Creating a supportive and predictable classroom setting can help Michael feel secure and reduce his stress, which can positively affect his focus and participation. **Incorrect Answer A**: While this may be well-intentioned, it could be inappropriate for Ms. Lee to discuss personal family matters directly with Michael without proper training and context. **Incorrect Answer B**: Although this may be a helpful step, it should not be the only action taken. Ms. Lee can provide immediate support within the classroom setting. **Incorrect Answer D**: While consistency is important, it is not the primary method for addressing the emotional and behavioral impacts of a family divorce.
10.	A, B, C & E	**Correct Answer A**: Keeping a reflective journal to document daily teaching experiences and student interactions helps teachers critically analyze and reflect on their practices and the dynamics in their classroom. **Correct Answer B**: Seeking feedback from colleagues through peer observations and discussions provides diverse perspectives and constructive suggestions for improvement. **Correct Answer C**: Reviewing and analyzing student performance data to identify areas for instructional improvement helps teachers understand the effectiveness of their instruction and make informed decisions. **Incorrect Answer D**: While communicating with parents is important, this does not directly serve as a self-assessment technique for the teacher. **Correct Answer E**: Attending professional development workshops and applying new strategies in the classroom offers new insights and methodologies that can enhance teaching practices.

This page intentionally left blank.

V. Content Pedagogy and Knowledge

Early childhood educators must be well-versed in national, state, and local learning standards to create and evaluate meaningful and challenging curricula for each child. This requires a comprehensive understanding of essential subject areas, including language and literacy, mathematics, science, social studies, and the arts, which form the foundation of children's learning competence.

Educators should be familiar with developmentally appropriate resources such as books, standards documents, web resources, and consultation with individuals possessing content expertise. These resources are critical for developing and implementing curricula that support children's diverse learning needs.

Furthermore, educators need to be knowledgeable about programs that support children with diverse needs, including at-risk children, English-language learners (ELLs), and children requiring early intervention. Understanding core concepts and standards in language, literacy, and mathematics is essential for making informed instructional decisions and effective pedagogical implementation.

The following concepts are discussed in this content category:

Language and Literacy

- Communication Concepts (Speaking, Listening, and Language)
- Developing Students' Emergent Reading Skills
- Developing Children's Comprehension of Literature and Informational Texts
- Integrating Literacy into Content Areas
- Developing Children's Writing Skills

Mathematics

- Operations and Algebraic Thinking
- Numbers and Operations in Base 10
- Measurement and Data
- Geometry in Early Childhood Education

Language and Literacy: Communication Concepts (Speaking, Listening, and Language)

Effective communication is foundational to early childhood education, encompassing speaking, listening, and language skills. As an educator, it is essential to understand strategies that support and enhance these communication concepts in young children.

Nonverbal Communication Cues

Nonverbal communication plays a crucial role in children's interactions and learning processes. Educators should be proficient in recognizing and using nonverbal cues to support communication development. These cues include facial expressions, gestures, body language, and eye contact. For example, a smile can convey encouragement, while pointing can help direct a child's attention. Teachers can model and teach children to interpret and use nonverbal signals effectively to enhance their understanding and engagement in the classroom.

Progression of Oral Language Development

Understanding the progression of oral language development is vital for setting realistic expectations and providing appropriate support. Oral language development typically follows a predictable sequence:

1. **Listening Comprehension**: Young children start by developing listening skills. They learn to recognize sounds, understand basic words, and follow simple instructions. Educators can foster listening comprehension by reading aloud, engaging in conversations, and using songs and rhymes.

2. **Verbal Communication**: As children's listening skills improve, they develop verbal communication abilities. This progression includes babbling, forming simple words, and constructing complete sentences. Encouraging children to express themselves, asking open-ended questions, and providing a language-rich environment can support this development.

Quick Tip

Monitor children's oral language development by regularly engaging them in conversations and interactive read-alouds. Use rich and varied vocabulary, ask open-ended questions, and provide immediate, supportive feedback to foster their language growth progressively.

3. **Advanced Language Skills**: Over time, children refine their language skills, including vocabulary expansion, proper grammar usage, and the ability to engage in more complex conversations. Educators should create opportunities for children to practice these skills through storytelling, role-playing, and group discussions.

Expectations for Listening Comprehension and Verbal Communication

It is essential to have clear expectations for children's listening comprehension and verbal communication at various developmental stages:

- **Infants and Toddlers**: Focus on responsive interactions, such as responding to coos and babbles and introducing simple words and phrases.

- **Preschoolers**: Encourage following multi-step instructions, expanding vocabulary, and forming basic sentences. Use interactive read-alouds and songs to reinforce comprehension.

- **Kindergarteners**: Support more complex sentence structures, storytelling, and active participation in group discussions. Provide opportunities for children to ask questions and express their thoughts.

By understanding and implementing these strategies, early childhood educators can effectively support and develop children's communication concepts, laying a strong foundation for their future academic and social success.

Facilitating Oral Language and Vocabulary Development

Effective strategies to facilitate and expand children's oral language and vocabulary are crucial for their overall language proficiency and academic success. Here are some key methods:

- **Rich Language Environment**: Create a language-rich classroom where children are exposed to various words and contexts. Use diverse vocabulary during instruction, read aloud, and engage in meaningful conversations.

- **Interactive Read-Alouds**: Use read-aloud sessions to introduce new vocabulary. Pause to explain unfamiliar words, ask questions, and encourage children to predict and retell parts of the story.

- **Word Walls**: Implement word walls to display new vocabulary words. Frequently reference and use these words in daily activities to reinforce their meaning and usage.

- **Vocabulary Games**: Incorporate games and activities, such as matching words with pictures, word bingo, and vocabulary scavenger hunts, to make learning new words engaging and fun.

Addressing Language Delays

Strategies to address language delays are essential to support children who may be struggling with their language development:

- **Early Identification and Intervention**: Regularly assess children's language skills to identify delays early. Collaborate with speech-language pathologists to develop intervention plans.

- **Individualized Instruction**: Tailor activities and instructions to meet the specific needs of children with language delays. Provide additional time, visual aids, and simplified language to support understanding.

- **Parental Involvement**: Engage parents in the intervention process by providing them with strategies and activities to practice at home, reinforcing language skills outside the classroom.

Developing Collaborative Conversation Skills

Encouraging children to participate in collaborative conversations enhances their communication skills and critical thinking:

- **Promoting Active Listening**: Teach children active listening skills, such as maintaining eye contact, nodding, and responding appropriately. Model these behaviors during classroom interactions.

- **Facilitating Discussions**: Organize and facilitate discussions by creating small groups where children can share their thoughts. Use prompts and questions to guide the conversation and ensure all children have the opportunity to contribute.

- **Constructing Questions**: Develop open-ended questions that promote critical thinking and deeper understanding. Encourage children to ask questions, express their opinions, and build on their peers' ideas.

Quick Tip

Create a classroom environment that encourages active listening and respectful dialogue. Use small group discussions and structured conversation prompts to help children practice taking turns, asking questions, and building on each other's ideas.

Developing Oral Presentation Skills

Strategies to develop children's oral presentation skills include:

- **Modeling**: Demonstrate effective speaking skills, such as clear articulation, appropriate volume, and confident body language. Encourage children to mimic these behaviors during their presentations.

- **Retelling**: Have children retell stories or events in their own words. This activity helps them organize their thoughts and practice sequencing and storytelling.

- **Practice Opportunities**: Provide frequent opportunities for children to present to their peers. Create a supportive environment where they can receive constructive feedback and improve their skills.

Promoting Technology Use for Story and Poem Recordings

Integrating technology into language learning can enhance children's engagement and creativity:

- **Digital Storytelling**: Use apps and software that allow children to create and record their own stories and poems. This activity combines technology with language skills and fosters creativity.

- **Classroom Blog or Podcast**: Set up a classroom blog or podcast where children can share their recordings with a wider audience. This platform encourages them to take pride in their work and improves their speaking and listening skills.

Understanding Standard English Grammar and Usage

Developing a solid understanding of the conventions of standard English grammar and usage is crucial for effective communication:

- **Explicit Instruction**: Teach grammar and usage rules explicitly through mini-lessons. Use examples from children's writing and speaking to illustrate correct and incorrect usage.

- **Practice and Application**: Provide ample opportunities for children to practice grammar skills in their writing and speaking. Use activities like sentence editing, grammar games, and peer reviews.

- **Feedback and Support**: Give constructive feedback on children's grammar and usage. Offer additional support and resources, such as grammar reference charts and interactive activities, to reinforce learning.

By employing these strategies, early childhood educators can effectively support and enhance children's communication skills, laying a strong foundation for their academic and social success.

Language and Literacy: Developing Students' Emergent Reading Skills

Emergent reading skills are crucial for young learners as they form the foundation for future literacy development. These skills include:

- Concepts of print,
- Phonological awareness
- Letter-sound knowledge
- Vocabulary
- Fluency

Quick Tip

To effectively develop emergent literacy skills in early childhood education, it is essential to implement explicit, systematic, and recursive instruction. Explicit instruction involves clearly and directly teaching specific reading skills, leaving no ambiguity for the learners. Systematic instruction refers to teaching these skills in a logical, sequential order, ensuring that each new skill builds upon previously learned skills. Recursive instruction involves regularly revisiting and reinforcing these skills to ensure mastery and retention.

Concepts of Print

Understanding concepts of print is a foundational skill for emergent readers. Teachers can develop children's concepts of print by:

- **Modeling Book Handling**: Demonstrate how to hold a book, turn pages from front to back, and follow text from left to right and top to bottom.

- **Interactive Read-Alouds**: Engage children in discussions about the parts of a book (cover, title, author, illustrator) and point out text features such as letters, words, and sentences.

- **Print-Rich Environment**: Create a classroom environment rich with print, including labeled objects, charts, and displays that encourage children to notice and interact with written language.

Phonological Awareness

Developing children's phonological awareness involves helping them recognize and manipulate the sounds in spoken language. Strategies include:

- **Rhyming Games**: Play games that involve identifying and producing rhyming words.
- **Syllable Clapping**: Practice breaking words into syllables by clapping or tapping for each syllable.
- **Sound Segmentation**: Teach children to segment words into individual sounds (phonemes) and blend sounds to form words.

Phonological Awareness vs. Phonemic Awareness

Phonological Awareness is an overarching skill that includes manipulating units of oral language, parts of words, syllables, onsets, and rimes. Students use their auditory and oral skills when engaging in phonological awareness.

Children who have phonological awareness can:

- Identify and make oral rhymes.
- Clap the number of syllables in a word.
- Recognize words with the same initial sounds as in *monkey* and *mother*.
- Recognize the sound of spoken language.
- Blend sounds (*bl, tr, sk*).
- Divide and manipulate words.

Phonemic Awareness is a subskill of phonological awareness. When students have phonemic awareness, they understand individual sounds (or phonemes) in words. For example, students who have phonemic awareness can separate the sounds in the word *cat* into three distinct phonemes: /k/, /æ/, and /t/.

When students engage in phonemic awareness activities, they use their oral and auditory skills. They do not have to see the word(s) to practice these skills. Both phonemic and phonological awareness are prerequisite skills to phonics.

Quick Tip

Think of phonological awareness as the umbrella encompassing identifying larger chunks of sounds in words: syllables, onsets, rimes, segments, etc. Phonemic awareness is a more nuanced skill requiring students to break up words by individual sounds rather than by large chunks of sounds. Both are essential foundational skills.

Letter-Sound Knowledge, Phonics, and Word-Analysis Skills

Building letter-sound knowledge and phonics skills is essential for decoding. Teachers can support this development through:

- **Alphabet Activities**: Use activities that help children recognize and name letters, both uppercase and lowercase.
- **Phonics Instruction**: Provide systematic and explicit instruction in letter-sound correspondences, blending, and segmenting sounds.
- **Word Analysis**: Teach children word-analysis skills, such as recognizing common word patterns (e.g., CVC, CVCC) and decoding unfamiliar words by applying phonics rules.
  - **CVC** – Consonant-vowel-consonant pattern as in the word *bat*.
  - **CVCC** – Consonant-vowel-consonant-consonant pattern as in the word *back*.
  - **CVCe** – Consonant-vowel-consonant-silent *e* pattern as in the word *make*.

Quick Tip

Phonics is sometimes referred to as letter-sound correspondence or grapheme-phoneme correspondence. Both terms mean the same thing: assigning a sound to a letter or groups of letters in a word.

The Alphabetic Principle

▼ **Pre-Alphabetic Phase**
Students read words by memorizing visual features or guessing words from context.

▼ **Partial-Alphabetic Phase**
Students recognize some letters and can use them to remember words by sight.

▼ **Full-Alphabetic Phase**
Readers possess extensive working knowledge of the graphophonemic system, and they can use this knowledge to analyze fully the connections between graphemes and phonemes in words. They can decode unfamiliar words and store fully analyzed sight words in memory.

▼ **Consolidated-Alphabetic Phase**
Students consolidate their knowledge of grapheme-phoneme blends into larger units that recur in different words.

The following example question is how this might look on the exam.

Example Problem

A teacher is using picture cards to help students recognize words. Students see the picture below and say, "Sun!" What phase of word recognition are the students in?

A. Pre-alphabetic

B. Partial- alphabetic

C. Full- alphabetic

D. Consolidated- alphabetic

Correct Answer: A

The students are only seeing a picture. Therefore, they are in the pre-alphabetic stage. Partial, full, and consolidated phases all require the use of letter recognition. In this case, there is only a picture.

Understand the connection between spoken and written language.

Oral language consists of 6 major areas: phonology, vocabulary, morphology, grammar, pragmatics, and discourse.

1. **Phonology** encompasses the organization of sounds in language.

2. **Vocabulary** (semantics) encompasses both expressive (speaking) and receptive (listening) vocabulary.

3. **Morphology** is the smallest units of meaning in words. An example of morphology is breaking up compound words and analyzing their meaning.

4. **Grammar** (syntax) is the structure of language and words.

5. **Pragmatics** focuses on the social cues or norms in language. This is often referred to as situations in language.

6. **Discourse** focuses on speaking and listening skills in language. Discourse means dialogue.

Vocabulary Development

Expanding children's vocabulary is crucial for reading comprehension and overall language development. Strategies include:

- **Read-Alouds**: Read a variety of texts aloud to children, introducing and discussing new vocabulary words.
- **Word Walls**: Create word walls with high-frequency words and thematic vocabulary that children can refer to and use in their writing and speaking.
- **Interactive Activities**: Engage children in activities that involve using new words in context, such as storytelling, drawing, and acting out meanings.

Determining Word Meaning

To develop children's ability to determine word meaning, teachers can use:

- **Context Clues**: Teach children to use context clues from the surrounding text to infer the meaning of unknown words. This is called semantic cueing.
- **Syntax and Grammar**: Help children understand how the structure of a sentence can provide clues to a word's meaning. This is called syntactic cueing.
- **Roots and Affixes**: Introduce common roots, prefixes, and suffixes to help children break down and understand complex words. This is called graphophonic cueing.

Fluency Development

Fluency is reading text accurately, quickly, and with expression, which supports comprehension. Teachers can promote fluency by:

- **Selecting Appropriate Texts**: Choose texts that are at the appropriate reading level for children to practice fluent reading.
- **Modeling Fluent Reading**: Demonstrate fluent reading through read-aloud sessions, showing how to read with proper intonation and expression.
- **Choral Reading and Repeated Reading**: Choral reading (reading together as a group) and repeated reading (reading the same text multiple times) can build children's reading confidence and fluency skills.

Language and Literacy: Developing Children's Comprehension of Literature and Informational Texts

To effectively develop children's comprehension abilities, it is essential to implement scaffolding strategies that support their progress toward independent, proficient reading. These strategies include providing access to grade-level texts and purposeful grouping and challenging students appropriately while they receive the support they need. Scaffolding techniques might involve modeling reading strategies, providing guided practice, and gradually releasing responsibility to the students as they become more capable readers.

Strategies for Developing Comprehension Skills

Several strategies can help children develop comprehension skills, including retelling and making text-to-self, text-to-world, and text-to-text connections. These strategies encourage children to relate the text to their own experiences, understand its relevance to the world, and draw parallels between texts.

- **Retelling** – Ask children to retell the main events in a story in their own words. This can be done through verbal storytelling, drawing pictures, or acting out the story. For example, after reading "The Very Hungry Caterpillar" by Eric Carle, children could retell the story by sequencing pictures of the caterpillar's different stages and the food it ate daily.
- **Text-to-Self Connections** – Encourage children to relate the text to their own experiences. After reading "Arthur's Tooth" by Marc Brown, ask children if they have ever lost a tooth and how they felt about it. This connection helps them relate personally to the story, making it more meaningful and memorable.

- **Text-to-World Connections** – Help children connect the text to larger world concepts or events. After reading "The Lorax" by Dr. Seuss, discuss environmental issues such as deforestation and pollution. Ask children if they have seen any news stories or documentaries about saving the environment, helping them connect the book's themes to real-world events.

- **Text-to-Text Connections** – Guide children to draw parallels between different texts. After reading "Charlotte's Web" by E.B. White, compare it with another story about animals, like "The Tale of Peter Rabbit" by Beatrix Potter. Discuss similarities and differences in the characters, settings, and plots, fostering an understanding of narrative structures and themes across different texts.

Monitoring Comprehension

Teaching children to monitor their comprehension is crucial for developing independent reading skills. Strategies such as making predictions, self-questioning, and summarizing can help children become more aware of their understanding and identify when they need to re-read or seek clarification. Tools such as think-alouds and graphic organizers can aid in this process by providing a visual representation of their thoughts and understanding.

Quick Tip

Metacognition, or thinking about thinking, is crucial for developing reading comprehension in young children. It helps them become aware of their thought processes while reading, improving their ability to understand and retain information. An effective strategy for fostering metacognition is the "Read Aloud, Think Aloud" approach, where teachers model their thought processes during reading, demonstrating how to monitor comprehension, make predictions, and clarify understanding.

Finding and Organizing Key Details and Main Ideas

Educators can use various strategies and tools to help children find and organize key details and main ideas in a text. Play-based activities, think-alouds, and graphic organizers can facilitate this process by making it interactive and engaging. These methods enable children to map out the main ideas and supporting details visually, enhancing their comprehension and retention of the text.

Common Graphic Organizers in Early Childhood Education

These graphic organizers aid in visual learning, helping young children to organize their thoughts and improve comprehension and critical thinking skills.

- **Venn Diagram** – Used to compare and contrast two or more items, ideas, or characters.

- **Story Map** – Helps outline the elements of a story, including setting, characters, problem, and solution.

- **KWL Chart (Know, Want to know, Learned)** – A tool to activate prior knowledge, set learning goals, and summarize what has been learned.

- **Sequence Chart** – Assists in understanding the order of events or steps in a process.

- **Web Diagram (Concept Map)** – Used to explore and organize ideas around a central concept or topic.

- **T-Chart** – Helps students organize information into two categories, such as pros and cons or facts and opinions.

- **Mind Map** – Encourages brainstorming by visually organizing information around a central idea with branches.

- **Cause and Effect Chart** – Used to identify the causes and effects of an event or situation.

Understanding Relationships Between Illustrations and Text

Lastly, teaching children to understand the relationships between illustrations, pictures, graphs, and the text in which they appear is essential for comprehensive reading. Strategies and tools such as discussing the illustrations, using graphic organizers, and drawing connections between visual elements and the text can help children grasp the full meaning of the content. This holistic approach ensures that children not only read the words but also understand the context and visual cues that enhance their comprehension.

Language and Literacy: Integrating Literacy into Content Areas

Integrating literacy into content areas such as mathematics, social studies, science, and the arts is essential for developing well-rounded, literate students. Effective strategies for integrating literacy across these subjects include:

1. **Mathematics**
    *   **Math Journals**: Encourage students to write about their problem-solving processes and mathematical thinking in journals.
    *   **Story Problems**: Use word problems that require reading comprehension and critical thinking to solve mathematical equations.
    *   **Math Literature**: Incorporate books and stories that include math concepts, such as "The Grapes of Math" by Greg Tang.

2. **Social Studies**
    *   **Historical Narratives**: Read and analyze historical stories and biographies to understand historical events and figures.
    *   **Primary Source Documents**: Use letters, diaries, and other primary sources to build reading and critical analysis skills.
    *   **Social Studies Journals**: Have students write reflections on historical events, cultural practices, and societal changes.

3. **Science**
    *   **Science Logs**: Students can document experiments, observations, and hypotheses in science logs.
    *   **Informational Texts**: Read and discuss nonfiction texts related to science topics, such as weather, plants, and animals.
    *   **Science Vocabulary**: Focus on the specific language and terminology used in science to build content-specific literacy.

4. **The Arts**
    *   **Art Critiques**: Encourage students to write about their interpretations and evaluations of artworks.
    *   **Drama and Script Writing**: Incorporate playwriting and performing scripts to enhance reading and writing skills.
    *   **Music and Lyrics**: Analyze song lyrics and their meanings, and write their own lyrics or poems inspired by music.

Developing an Understanding of Features and Structures of Text Across Genres

Children need to understand texts' different features and structures across various genres to enhance their comprehension and appreciation of literature. Strategies include:

*   **Genre Exploration**: Introduce children to various genres, including fiction, nonfiction, poetry, and drama. Discuss the unique characteristics of each genre.

- **Text Structure Analysis**: Teach children to identify and understand common text structures such as cause and effect, compare and contrast, sequence, and problem and solution. Use graphic organizers to map these structures.

- **Feature Identification**: Highlight and discuss features such as headings, subheadings, captions, diagrams, and glossaries in informational texts to help children navigate and comprehend content.

Developing an Understanding of Point of View

Understanding point of view is crucial for comprehending and analyzing texts. Strategies to develop this understanding include:

- **Character Perspectives**: Use stories with multiple characters and discuss how each character's perspective influences the narrative. Ask questions like, "How might this story change if told by a different character?"

- **Author's Point of View**: Teach children to recognize the author's perspective and purpose in fiction and nonfiction texts. Discuss why the author might have chosen to write from a particular viewpoint.

- **Comparing Points of View**: Read different texts on the same topic and compare how the points of view differ. Use Venn diagrams or other graphic organizers to represent these differences visually.

Quick Tip

When taking the exam, keep an eye out for the phrase *content-area reading strategies*. These strategies, such as using math journals, historical narratives, science logs, and art critiques, are often the correct answers. They emphasize integrating literacy skills across different subjects, a key concept in effective early childhood education.

Educators can create a rich, interdisciplinary learning environment that fosters comprehensive literacy development in young children by integrating literacy into content areas and focusing on the understanding of text features, structures, and points of view.

Language and Literacy: Developing Children's Writing Skills

Developing writing skills in early childhood education is crucial for laying the foundation for literacy and communication. Writing not only enhances children's ability to express their thoughts and ideas but also supports their reading skills, as the processes are closely interconnected.

Writing in early childhood fosters fine motor skills, critical thinking, and creativity. Through various writing activities, children learn to organize their thoughts, develop logical sequences, and convey information effectively. Encouraging children to write also builds their confidence and self-esteem as they see their progress and realize the power of their words.

Developmental Stages of Writing

Understanding the developmental stages of writing helps educators tailor their instruction to meet children's needs at each stage:

1. **Scribbling**: Children make random marks on paper, the earliest form of writing. They may not yet understand that writing conveys meaning.

2. **Drawing and Symbolic Writing**: Children draw pictures and may begin to use symbols or letter-like forms to represent words and ideas.

3. **Random Letters and Letter Strings**: Children write strings of random letters, often without spaces, to imitate writing. They may begin to include some recognizable letters.

4. **Beginning Sounds**: Children write the initial sounds of words and start to recognize that letters correspond to sounds.

5. **Phonetic Spelling**: Children spell words the way they sound, often leaving out letters but showing an understanding of phonetics.

6. **Transitional Spelling**: Children begin to spell words more conventionally, mixing phonetic and correct spelling.

7. **Conventional Spelling:** Children consistently use correct spelling, punctuation, and grammar in their writing.

Approaches to Writing Instruction

Developing children's writing skills is a critical component of early childhood education. Writing instruction should be seen as a cyclical process that includes planning, drafting, revising, editing, and publishing. Different approaches to writing instruction include:

- **Interactive Writing**: Teachers and students compose text together, with the teacher guiding and modeling the writing process.
- **Shared Writing**: The teacher writes while the students contribute ideas, helping them see the connection between thought and the written word.
- **Independent Writing**: Students write independently on self-chosen or assigned topics, practicing their learned skills.

Strategies to Guide Planning for Writing

Effective writing instruction involves guiding students in the planning phase. Strategies include:

- **Brainstorming**: Encourage students to generate ideas before writing.
- **Graphic Organizers**: Use tools like story maps, Venn diagrams, and webs to help students organize their thoughts.
- **Writing Prompts**: Provide prompts to stimulate thinking and guide writing tasks.

Using Technology to Produce and Publish Writing

Technology can enhance the writing process by providing tools for production and publication:

- **Word Processors**: Use programs like Microsoft Word or Google Docs to help children type and edit their work.
- **Publishing Tools**: Introduce platforms such as blogs or classroom websites where students can publish their writing for a broader audience.
- **Digital Storytelling**: Use apps and software that allow students to create and share digital stories, integrating text, images, and sound.

Supporting Drawing as a Form of Writing

Drawing is a vital form of expression for young children and can be an early step in the writing process:

- **Drawing and Writing**: Encourage children to draw pictures related to their writing topics to help them organize their thoughts and ideas.
- **Labeling Drawings**: Have children label their drawings with words or short sentences, connecting visual art with written language.
- **Storytelling through Pictures**: Use picture books and ask children to create their own stories through sequential drawings.

Supporting the Development of Handwriting

Good handwriting is essential for clear communication and involves developing fine motor skills:

- **Manipulatives**: Use a variety of tools, such as playdough, tweezers, and pegboards, to strengthen the fine motor skills necessary for writing.
- **Handwriting Practice**: Provide practice with tracing, copying, and freehand writing of letters and words.
- **Special Grips**: Use pencil grips and other adaptive tools to help children correctly hold writing instruments.

Developing Knowledge of Different Writing Types

Children should be familiar with the purposes and structures of different types of writing:

- **Opinion Writing**: Teach children to express their preferences or opinions about a topic, providing reasons and examples.
- **Informative/Explanatory Writing**: Guide children in writing facts and information about a topic, explaining concepts clearly.
- **Narrative Writing**: Encourage children to write stories with a clear sequence of events, including characters, settings, and plots.

Mathematics: Counting and Cardinality

Counting and cardinality are fundamental concepts in early childhood mathematics education. Developing these skills in young children lays the foundation for more advanced mathematical understanding. Teaching counting involves helping children learn number names, the count sequence, and the ability to count objects accurately. Cardinality, the understanding that the last number counted represents the total quantity of objects, is crucial for grasping the true meaning of numbers.

Developing Children's Knowledge of Number Names and the Count Sequence

Early childhood educators are critical in helping children develop foundational mathematics skills. One of the first steps is teaching number names and the count sequence. Strategies include:

- **Number Songs and Rhymes**: Use songs and rhymes to help children memorize number names and sequences.
- **Counting Books**: Read books focusing on counting to reinforce number names and order.
- **Daily Counting Practice**: Incorporate counting into daily routines, such as counting steps, snacks, or classmates.

Understanding the Relationship Between Number Names and Quantities

Connecting counting to cardinality involves helping children understand that the last number name said when counting objects represents the total number of objects. Techniques include:

- **Hands-On Counting Activities**: Provide objects for children to count, emphasizing the total number after counting each set.
- **Counting Games**: Play games that involve counting objects and stating the total, reinforcing the concept of cardinality.
- **Questioning Techniques**: Ask questions like, "How many blocks do you have?" after they have counted them to make the connection between counting and quantity clear.

Using Counting to Determine Quantities in Various Configurations

Children need to learn how to count objects in different arrangements, such as lines, rectangular arrays, and circles. Educators can use the following strategies:

- **Structured Activities**: Arrange objects in various configurations and have children count them, discussing how the arrangement does not change the total number.
- **Visual Aids**: Use visual aids like counting mats or grids to help children see and count objects in different patterns.
- **Interactive Counting**: Encourage children to rearrange objects themselves and count them in each new configuration to reinforce the concept.

Developing the Ability to Compare Numbers

Comparing numbers involves understanding more than, less than, and equal to relationships. Strategies include:

- **Number Comparisons**: Use objects or number cards to compare quantities and numbers, discussing which is more, less, or if they are equal.
- **Interactive Activities**: Create games where children compare groups of objects, such as "Who has more?" or "Are these groups equal?"
- **Visual Representations**: Use visual tools like number lines or charts to compare numbers and quantities.

Strategies and Tools to Support Learning in Counting

Various strategies and tools can enhance children's understanding of counting and cardinality:

- **Manipulatives**: Use counting manipulatives such as blocks, beads, or counters to make counting tangible and interactive.
- **Place Value Mats**: Introduce place value mats to help children understand the position and value of numbers.
- **Hundreds Charts**: Use hundreds charts for children to practice counting and recognizing number patterns.
- **Interactive Technology**: Incorporate educational apps and software for interactive counting exercises and games.

Quick Tip

On the exam, look for strategies integrating hands-on activities, visual aids, and interactive learning tools to teach counting and cardinality. These approaches are often the correct answers, emphasizing active engagement and concrete understanding of mathematical concepts.

Mathematics: Operations and Algebraic Thinking

Operations and algebraic thinking in early childhood lay the groundwork for future mathematical learning and problem-solving. At this stage, children begin to develop strategies and algorithms for basic operations such as addition and subtraction through hands-on activities and visual aids like number lines and manipulatives.

Understanding patterns and their rules fosters early algebraic thinking while exploring operations on rational numbers helps transition from concrete to abstract mathematical concepts. Teachers play a crucial role in addressing common misconceptions and using various methods, including mental math and word problems, to deepen children's understanding. By integrating these strategies, educators help young learners build a solid foundation in mathematical operations and thinking skills.

Supporting the Development of Strategies and Algorithms for Addition and Subtraction

Developing children's understanding of addition and subtraction is fundamental to early mathematics education. Teachers can support this development by:

- **Using Manipulatives**: Provide concrete objects like counters, blocks, or beads for children to add and subtract physically.
- **Visual Aids**: Utilize number lines and ten frames to help children visualize addition and subtraction processes.
- **Story Problems**: Create simple word problems that require addition and subtraction, encouraging children to use strategies like counting on, counting back, and using known facts.
- **Interactive Activities**: Engage children in games and activities that involve adding and subtracting, such as board games or card games.

Developing Understanding of Patterns

Recognizing and understanding patterns is crucial for mathematical thinking. Strategies to develop this understanding include:

- **Pattern Recognition**: Use everyday objects (e.g., colored blocks, beads, or shapes) to create and identify patterns.
- **Pattern Extension**: Encourage children to extend patterns and predict what comes next.
- **Pattern Creation**: Have children create their own patterns using various materials and explain the rules governing them.

Understanding the prerequisite skills needed for future mathematical development

As students progress in learning math, they move from understanding concrete concepts to grasping more abstract ideas. This developmental journey is akin to learning any new subject, beginning with tangible, hands-on experiences and advancing towards abstract thinking.

Use the acronym **CRA.**

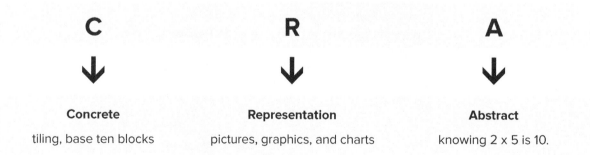

C	R	A
↓	↓	↓
Concrete	**Representation**	**Abstract**
tiling, base ten blocks	pictures, graphics, and charts	knowing 2 x 5 is 10.

Math Fluency

Fluency in elementary mathematics relates to the speed and accuracy by which a student can answer a basic math fact. Math fact fluency is a four-step process.

- **Accuracy** – Solving problems using the correct method and arriving at the correct answer. This step relates to a student's understanding, not speed or recall.
- **Automaticity** – Exploring efficient strategies for finding the correct answer. Students achieving automaticity can give a correct answer as an automatic response.
- **Rate** – Working toward quick recall of a math fact. Students who are fluent in math facts can respond to an answer at a quick rate.
- **Flexibility** – Choosing and explaining different strategies for arriving at a correct answer. This step relates to a student's deep understanding, not speed or recall.

Educators must understand the prerequisite skills for future math skills when teaching foundational math skills.

Recognizing patterns

Recognizing, analyzing, and applying different methods for teaching mathematical concepts and procedures is essential in building math skills. Students must be able to understand that a repeating core pattern of the shapes looks like this:

One-to-one correspondence

One-to-one correspondence is a counting and quantity principle that refers to the understanding that each object in a group can be counted once and only once. It is useful in the early stages for children to tag or touch each item being counted and to move it out of the way as it is counted. This is usually done using manipulatives or physical objects.

Grouping and classification by one or more attributes

Students must learn to group and sort objects based on attributes. An example activity might be having students grab a handful of blue and green tiles and then fill out the sentences below.

- I have _____ blue tiles.
- I have _____ green tiles.
- I have more _____ tiles than _____ tiles.
- I have _____ tiles in all.

Subitizing

Subitizing is the ability to instantly recognize the number of objects in a small group without counting them. This skill is foundational in early math development, as it helps children understand quantities and develop number sense. For example, when a child sees a group of three apples, they can immediately recognize there are three without counting each apple individually. When a child sees the dots on a pair of dice, they can automatically identify the number of dots without counting them.

Sequencing and conservation of numbers

Understanding sequences of numbers helps children recognize patterns and make sense of the world.

For example, a student fills out the missing numbers in the picture below.

1		3			6		8		10

Conservation of numbers means that a person can understand that the number of objects remains the same even when rearranged.

For example, the groups below represent four objects regardless of their arrangement.

Simple directions related to position and proximity

Students should be able to relate positions using proximity. Below is an example.

Describe the position of the square in the picture below.

The square is smaller and is above the triangle.

Represents numbers in multiple ways

Students in early childhood grades will represent numbers in different ways: shapes, tallies, objects, words, etc. See the example below.

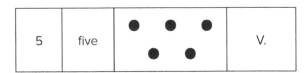

Uses Counting and Cardinality Principles

There are five long-established counting principles that children must understand to count effectively. These principles are:

1. **Stable Order** – Understanding the verbal sequence of counting; being able to say the number names in the correct sequential order.

2. **One-to-One Correspondence** – Understanding that each object receives one count and only one count when saying the number names in sequence.

3. **Cardinality** – Understanding that the last number spoken in a counting sequence represents the quantity of that set.

4. **Abstraction** – Understanding that the quantity of items does not change based on their characteristics or what is being counted. For example, any set of objects, regardless of color, shape, or size, can be counted as a group. This principle also applies to non-physical things, such as sounds or imaginary objects, demonstrating that the counting process remains consistent regardless of the items being counted.

5. **Order Irrelevance** – Knowing that the order in which items are counted is irrelevant—whether left-to-right, right-to-left, or in a random fashion—if every object in the set is given one count and only one count.

Compensation Strategy for Addition

The compensation strategy is a helpful technique for simplifying the process of adding numbers, especially for young learners. It involves adjusting one of the numbers to make the addition easier and compensating for that adjustment to find the correct answer. This method helps children understand the flexibility and properties of numbers, enhancing their mental math skills.

Example:

Suppose we need to add 9 and 6.

1. **Adjust One Number:** Round one number to a more convenient value. Here, we can round 9 up to 10.

2. **Add the Adjusted Numbers:** Add the rounded number to the other number.

$$10 + 6 = 16$$

3. **Compensate for the Adjustment:** Since we added one extra (rounding nine up to 10), we need to subtract one from the result to get the correct answer.

$$16 - 1 = 15$$

Thus, using the compensation strategy, 9 + 6 = 15

This technique speeds up mental calculations and helps young children better understand number properties and arithmetic operations.

Using Manipulatives

Early childhood education students can use manipulatives to represent abstract mathematical concepts. There are many different types of math manipulatives. The following are a few that are helpful for young learners.

Example:

Model the problem below using both a manipulative and a number line.

Dory has five books. Kelvin gives her four more books. How many books does Dory have now?

Solution: This problem is an add-to problem where the total is unknown. Using snap cubes, we can start with five and then add four more to the five to find the total. Students conclude that there are nine total cubes.

ADDEND	ADDEND	SUM

Using a number line, start with the first addend, five, then move four spaces right to find the total number of books.

Example: Use groups and arrays to model the problem below.

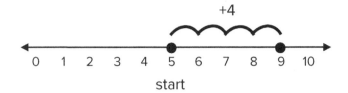

Example: Tina ordered four boxes of tennis balls. Each box contains three tennis balls. How many tennis balls did Tina order?

Solution: To use groups, show three tennis balls in each of the four boxes. Students should see that repeated addition is the same as multiplication, and four groups of three equals 12.

An array puts groups into organized lines, preparing students for additional math topics, such as area. The process and result are the same as those of the groups. There are four rows of three tennis balls each, which is 12.

Area model

Area models, linear models, and set models are different ways to represent fraction problems physically.

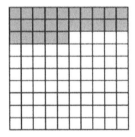

In an area model, fractions are represented as part of a region. Think of a ten-by-ten grid with some of the squares shaded. The shaded squares represent a fractional part of the whole.

Linear model

In a linear model, the lengths of objects are compared.

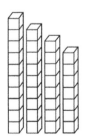

For example, imagine four red snap cubes snapped together in a row and three green snap cubes snapped together to form another row. The green cubes are three-fourths the length of the red cubes.

Set model

In a set model, a number of individual objects make up one whole.

For example, eight, two-color counters could make up 1 set of counters; then four counters would represent $\frac{4}{8}$ or $\frac{1}{2}$ of the set.

Understanding Operations on Rational Numbers

Operations on rational numbers in a first-grade classroom involve performing basic arithmetic operations such as addition and subtraction on numbers that can be expressed as simple fractions.

Unit Fraction	Manipulative Representation	Number Line Representation
$\frac{1}{2}$	A circle divided into two halves each labeled $\frac{1}{2}$, or a rectangle divided into two halves each labeled $\frac{1}{2}$	The fraction $\frac{1}{2}$ is the same distance from both 0 and 1.
$\frac{1}{4}$	A circle divided into four quarters each labeled $\frac{1}{4}$, or a rectangle divided into four quarters each labeled $\frac{1}{4}$	The fraction $\frac{1}{4}$ is closer to 0 than 1, and $\frac{1}{4}$ is less than $\frac{1}{2}$.
$\frac{1}{5}$	A circle divided into five parts each labeled $\frac{1}{5}$, or a rectangle divided into five parts each labeled $\frac{1}{5}$	The fraction $\frac{2}{5}$ is closer to 0 than 1, and $\frac{3}{5}$ is greater than $\frac{1}{2}$.

Building an understanding of operations on rational numbers requires moving from concrete to abstract concepts. Effective methods include:

- **Concrete Methods**: Use manipulatives like fraction bars or area models to represent operations on rational numbers.
- **Visual Methods**: Employ number lines and diagrams to show addition, subtraction, multiplication, and division of rational numbers.
- **Word Problems**: Incorporate arithmetic and word problems that require operations on rational numbers, emphasizing real-world applications.

Addressing Misconceptions

Children often develop misconceptions about mathematical concepts, such as the conservation of numbers. Strategies to address these include:

- **Diagnostic Assessment**: Use assessments to identify specific misconceptions.
- **Targeted Instruction**: Provide clear explanations and activities that address and correct misconceptions.
- **Concept Reinforcement**: Reinforce correct concepts through repeated practice and varied examples.

Developing Understanding of Patterns

Developing an understanding of patterns involves:

- **Generating Rules**: Teach children to identify the rule governing a pattern and to apply this rule to generate subsequent terms.
- **Exploring Patterns**: Use different contexts, such as number patterns, shape patterns, and repeating sequences, to broaden children's understanding.

Quick Tip

When studying operations and algebraic thinking, look for strategies emphasizing hands-on activities, visual representations, and real-world applications. Exam questions often highlight these approaches and are key to building a deep understanding of mathematical concepts in young learners.

Mathematics: Numbers and Operations in Base 10

Place value is a critical concept for understanding numbers and operations. Strategies to develop this understanding include:

- **Place Value Charts**: Use charts to help children see the value of each digit in a number.
- **Manipulatives**: Utilize base-ten blocks or place value disks to represent numbers physically.
- **Expanded Form**: Teach children to write numbers in expanded form to highlight the value of each digit.

Representations of Rational Numbers and Their Properties

To develop children's understanding of rational numbers and their properties, teachers can:

- **Comparison Strategies**: Use visual aids and symbols (<, >, =) to compare rational numbers.
- **Number Lines**: Represent rational numbers on number lines to show their relative positions and distances.
- **Equivalent Fractions**: Teach children about equivalent fractions using area models and fraction strips.

The value of a certain digit is determined by the place it resides in a number. In our number system, each "place" has a value of ten times the place to its right or 1/10 of the number to its left. The place value of each digit in a number is included in the word form of a number.

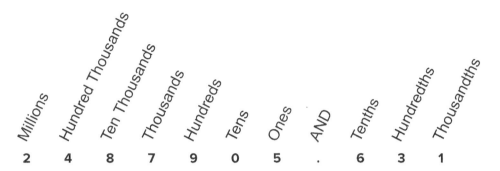

For example, the number 2,487,905.631 is read as:

Two million, four hundred eighty-seven thousand, nine hundred five, and six hundred thirty-one thousandths.

Knowledge of place value helps students compose and decompose larger numbers to understand the numbers' sizes better. Knowing how to manipulate a number using the base ten system is essential in building mathematical skills. Moving the decimal point to the left (to create a smaller number) is the same as dividing by increments of 10 or multiplying by increments of $\frac{1}{10}$. Conversely, moving the decimal point to the right (to create a larger number) is the same as multiplying by increments of 10. Increments of 10 include 10, 100, 1000, 10,000...etc.

Mathematics: Measurement and Data in Early Childhood Education

Measurement and data skills are essential components of early childhood education, providing young learners with the foundational tools they need to understand the world around them.

Teaching measurement involves helping children describe and compare attributes such as length, weight, and volume using both nonstandard and standard units. Activities like measuring objects with paperclips or using a balance scale to compare weights make these concepts accessible and engaging.

Data skills involve collecting, representing, and interpreting information through tools like bar graphs and pictographs. By organizing and analyzing data, children develop critical thinking and problem-solving skills. Educators can make measurement and data meaningful and relevant by incorporating hands-on activities and real-life applications, setting the stage for more advanced mathematical learning.

Describing and Comparing Attributes of Objects

Developing children's ability to describe and compare attributes of objects is foundational in early childhood mathematics. Educators can facilitate this by providing various objects and encouraging children to explore and discuss attributes such as size, weight, length, and color. Activities like sorting objects by size or comparing the weights of different items using a balance scale help children understand and articulate these attributes.

Classifying Objects into Categories

Classifying objects into given categories enhances children's cognitive and organizational skills. Teachers can create activities where children sort objects based on shape, color, or other attributes. For instance, children can classify a mix of blocks into categories of circles, squares, and triangles, which helps them recognize patterns and organize information systematically.

Measuring and Estimating Lengths in Nonstandard Units

Introducing children to measurement through nonstandard units makes the concept accessible and engaging. Teachers can measure lengths using everyday objects like paperclips, blocks, or hand spans. For example, children can measure the length of a desk using paperclips and then compare their results. This hands-on approach helps children understand the concept of measurement and estimation tangibly.

Identifying and Representing Time

Helping children identify and represent time involves familiarizing them with analog and digital clocks and concepts of past, present, and future. Teachers can use tools like classroom schedules, visual timers, and daily routines to teach time-related skills. Activities like sequencing events in a day or using timers for activities can reinforce their understanding of time.

Representing and Interpreting Data

Introducing children to data representation and interpretation can be both fun and educational. Teachers can use simple tools like bar graphs, pictographs, and charts to help children visualize and understand data. For instance, children can collect data on their favorite fruits and then represent this information in a bar graph. Discussing the results helps them interpret the data and draw conclusions, fostering critical thinking skills.

Manipulative Representations		
Attribute blocks	• Sorting • Patterns • Attributes of figures	
Base-10 blocks	• Place value • Whole number operations • Comparing numbers • Regrouping with addition and subtraction • Area and volume	
Bar diagram	• Solve for an unknown value using one of the four operations • Solve word problems	Kelly added 6 more stamps to her collection. Now she has 18 stamps. How many did she have before? 18 | ? | 6 |
Counters	• Sorting • Counting	

Manipulative Representations		
Geoboard	• Perimeter • Area • Properties of basic shapes • Congruency and Similarity	
Paperclips	• Can be used to measure objects • One paperclip is one unit of measure	
Fraction strips	• Perform operations with fractions • Represent fractional parts	 $$1/_2 = 1/_4 + 1/_4 = 1/_8 + 1/_8 + 1/_8 + 1/_8$$
Snap cubes	• Combine like terms • Represent ratios • Distributive property • Multiply polynomials • Factoring polynomials	
Tiles	• Perform operations with fractions • Represent fractional parts	
Graphs	• Represent data • Compare data	

Mathematics: Geometry in Early Childhood Education

Geometry in early childhood education focuses on helping young learners develop an understanding of shapes and spatial relationships. Children build a foundational knowledge of geometric concepts by engaging in activities that involve identifying, describing, and analyzing shapes.

Identifying and Describing Shapes

Identifying and describing shape attributes are essential prerequisite skills for geometry. This foundational skill can be fostered through activities that involve recognizing and naming various shapes in the environment, such as circles, squares, triangles, and rectangles. Teachers can use shape-sorting games, shape hunts, and interactive storybooks focusing on shapes to reinforce this skill. Additionally, incorporating songs and rhymes about shapes can make learning engaging and memorable.

Figure	Name	Number of Sides
	Triangle	3
	Rectangle	4
	Square	4
	Pentagon	5
	Hexagon	6
	Heptagon	7
	Octagon	8

Analyzing, Comparing, Creating, and Composing Shapes

Children should also be encouraged to analyze and compare shapes, understanding their properties and differences. Activities that involve sorting shapes by attributes, such as the number of sides or corners, can aid in this understanding. Creating and composing shapes using tools like pattern blocks or tangrams helps children see how smaller shapes can come together to form larger shapes. Drawing and constructing shapes with various materials like clay or straws allows for hands-on learning and creativity.

Figure Name	Image	Attributes
Rectangle		• All angles equal • Opposite sides have the same length • A special type of parallelogram • Opposite sides are parallel
Square		• All angles equal • All sides have the same length • A special type of parallelogram • A special type of rectangle • Opposite sides are parallel
Circle		• Diameter goes through the center of the circle to the edge of the circle • Radius starts at the center of the circle and ends on the edge of the circle • The radius is half the length of the diameter.
Cube		• All sides of a cube are squares • All sides have the same length • All angles equal

Understanding Characteristics of One-, Two-, and Three-Dimensional Figures

Introducing children to the characteristics of one-, two-, and three-dimensional figures helps them make connections between abstract concepts and real-world objects. Using concrete and virtual manipulatives, such as building blocks, geometric solids, and interactive software, can enhance this understanding. For example, children can explore how a square can become a cube or how a circle can become a sphere. Real-world connections, such as identifying shapes in the classroom or during outdoor activities, help solidify these concepts.

Using Mathematical Vocabulary and Definitions

Developing mathematical vocabulary is crucial for children to describe figures accurately and to understand similarities and differences among one-, two-, and three-dimensional figures. Teachers can introduce terms such as "side," "corner," "edge," "face," and "vertex" through interactive discussions and visual aids. Encouraging children to use these terms during activities, such as describing a drawing or explaining a construction, reinforces their understanding. Story problems and guided questioning can also prompt children to use mathematical vocabulary in context.

The table that follows lists the names of prisms and pyramids and gives an example of a possible net. Sometimes, the figure is turned on its side, and the bases are located on the sides of the figure (see the rectangular prism and triangular figures in the table).

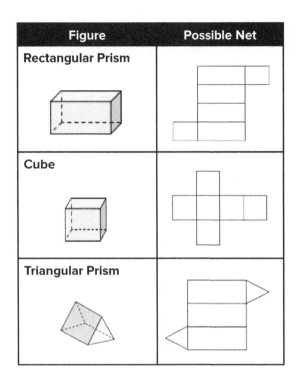

Figure	Possible Net
Rectangular Prism	
Cube	
Triangular Prism	

Figure	Possible Net
Square Pyramid	
Triangular Pyramid	
Cylinder	

Quick Tip

Teachers can create an immersive and enjoyable learning environment that promotes early geometric thinking by incorporating songs, rhymes, and interactive storybooks focused on shapes. Overall, early exposure to geometry supports children's cognitive development and prepares them for more advanced mathematical concepts in the future.

Content Pedagogy and Knowledge – Practice Questions

1. When students can identify phonemes in words, segment words into syllables and onset-rime, and blend sounds in words, they are demonstrating:

   A. Phonological awareness

   B. Phonics mastery

   C. Phonemic awareness

   D. Structural analysis

2. Phonemic awareness includes the ability to:

   A. Form compound words and combine word parts.

   B. Spell accurately and decode unfamiliar words.

   C. Pronounce individual sounds in words.

   D. Differentiate between homonyms and spell them accurately.

3. Which literacy skill involves hearing, identifying, and manipulating individual sounds in spoken words and is crucial for developing reading proficiency?

   A. Phonemic awareness

   B. Phonics

   C. Sentence decoding

   D. Word families

4. Which literacy concept focuses on recognizing common patterns in groups of words, such as -at, -an, and -in, to help children develop reading and spelling skills?

   A. Root words

   B. Word families

   C. Phonemic awareness

   D. Sentence decoding

5. How does phonics instruction contribute to literacy development in young children?

   A. By teaching the meaning of root words and their derivatives

   B. By helping children understand and use grammatical structures in sentences

   C. By teaching the relationships between letters and sounds, enabling children to decode words

   D. By promoting the recognition and manipulation of individual sounds in spoken language

6. Mr. Jones is designing a lesson for a second-grade class to introduce the mathematical concept of geometry, which requires thoughtful planning and evaluation. Which instructional strategies best support this goal, and how could Mr. Jones evaluate the lesson's effectiveness?

   A. Use a lecture to explain different geometric shapes and follow up with a written test.

   B. Have students complete a worksheet identifying shapes, then grade the worksheet to assess understanding.

   C. Introduce shapes using manipulatives and interactive activities, then assess understanding through student participation and a hands-on project.

   D. Show a video about shapes and a multiple-choice quiz to evaluate comprehension.

7. Before introducing a lesson on addition to first-grade students, what prior experiences should they have been exposed to?

   A. Identifying and naming geometric shapes.

   B. Recognizing and counting numbers up to 20.

   C. Understanding basic subtraction.

   D. Using an array to represent multiplication.

8. Ms. Carter wants to develop her preschool students' ability to identify and describe shapes. Which of the following activities would best support this goal?

   ☐ A. Have students trace shapes with stencils and then color them in.

   ☐ B. Use shape-sorting games where students match shapes to their corresponding outlines.

   ☐ C. Read a storybook that features shapes prominently and ask students to point out and name shapes as they appear.

   ☐ D. Take students on a shape hunt around the classroom to find and identify various shapes in their environment.

   ☐ E. Drawing pictures of shapes on the board and asking students to copy them into their notebooks.

9. A first-grade teacher goes over place value with students. The teacher emphasizes that moving the decimal point to the left (to create a smaller number) is the same as dividing by which of the following?

   A. 2

   B. 5

   C. 100

   D. 10

10. A first-grade teacher wants to introduce students to measurement. Which of the following activities would be most appropriate for this purpose?

   A. Ask students to use a ruler to measure the length of their desks in inches.

   B. Have students estimate the length of their desks using their hands.

   C. Show a video on different units of measurement.

   D. Use paperclips to measure the length of students' desks and record the results.

Number	Answer	Explanation
1.	A	**Correct Answer A**: Phonological awareness is the ability to break words down by large units of sounds in words—onset and rime, syllables, **Incorrect Answer B:** Phonics is letter-sound correspondence and requires students to see the word and decode it. **Incorrect Answer C:** Phonemic awareness is ability to split words into individual sounds or phonemes, which is crucial for spelling and sounding out words. This does not include larger chunks of words as described in the question. **Incorrect Answer D:** Structural analysis includes breaking words apart by prefixes, suffixes, and compound words. This falls under phonics, not phonological awareness.
2.	C	**Correct Answer C:** Phonemic awareness involves only listening to and pronouncing sounds in words. In fact, students can practice phonemic awareness without any paper or pencils. It is only the individual sounds (phonemes) in words. All the other answer choices emphasize letter-sound correspondence and spelling, which is phonics.
3.	A	**Correct Answer A:** Phonemic awareness involves the ability to hear, identify, and manipulate individual sounds (phonemes) in spoken words. It is a crucial foundational skill for developing reading proficiency, as it helps children understand that words are made up of smaller sounds. **Incorrect Answer B** Phonics is related to the relationship between letters and sounds but does not involve the manipulation of sounds in spoken words. **Incorrect Answer C:** Sentence decoding involves understanding and interpreting sentences, which is a higher-level skill that builds on phonemic awareness and phonics. **Incorrect Answer D:** Word families are groups of words with a common feature or pattern, typically used to help with reading and spelling.
4.	B	**Correct Answer B:** Word families focus on the recognition of common patterns in groups of words, such as -at, -an, and -in. This helps children develop reading and spelling skills by recognizing familiar chunks within words. **Incorrect Answer A:** Root words are the base form of words, which can be expanded with prefixes and suffixes, but this concept is broader than word families. **Incorrect Answer C:** Phonemic awareness involves the manipulation of individual sounds in spoken words, not recognizing word patterns. **Incorrect Answer D:** Sentence decoding involves interpreting sentences, which relies on understanding individual words and their meanings.

Number	Answer	Explanation
5.	C	**Correct Answer C:** Phonics instruction contributes to literacy development by teaching the relationships between letters and sounds, enabling children to decode words. This helps children read unfamiliar words by sounding them out. **Incorrect Answer A:** Teaching the meaning of root words and their derivatives is more related to vocabulary development than phonics instruction. **Incorrect Answer B:** Understanding and using grammatical structures in sentences pertains to syntax, which is a separate aspect of language development. **Incorrect Answer: D:** Promoting the recognition and manipulation of individual sounds in spoken language is a component of phonemic awareness, not phonics.
6.	C	**Correct Answer C:** Introducing shapes using manipulatives and interactive activities helps engage students and allows them to explore geometric concepts hands-on. Evaluating understanding through student participation and a hands-on project provides a comprehensive assessment of their grasp of the concepts. **Incorrect Answer A:** Using a lecture to explain shapes might not be engaging for second graders, and a written test may not accurately assess their understanding. **Incorrect Answer B:** While worksheets can be useful, they do not provide interactive and exploratory experiences that help young children understand geometric concepts deeply. **Incorrect Answer D:** Videos can be engaging, but relying solely on a multiple-choice quiz may not capture students' ability to apply and explore geometric concepts actively.
7.	B	**Correct Answer B:** Recognizing and counting numbers up to 20 is essential for students before learning addition, as it provides them with the foundational number sense needed to understand combining quantities. **Incorrect Answer A:** While identifying and naming geometric shapes is important, it is not directly related to the foundational skills needed for addition. **Incorrect Answer C:** Understanding basic subtraction is typically introduced after addition, so it would not be a prerequisite experience. **Incorrect Answer D:** Using an array to represent multiplication is a skill that is more advanced and not necessary before learning basic addition.

Number	Answer	Explanation
8.	B, C, and D	**Correct Answer B:** Using shape-sorting games where students match shapes to their corresponding outlines directly engages students in recognizing and naming various shapes, reinforcing their ability to identify and describe shapes. **Correct Answer C:** Reading a storybook that features shapes prominently and asking students to point out and name shapes as they appear integrates literacy with shape recognition, helping students identify and describe shapes within the context of a story. **Correct Answer D:** Taking students on a shape hunt around the classroom to find and identify various shapes in their environment encourages students to explore their environment and apply their knowledge of shapes in a real-world context, reinforcing their ability to identify and describe shapes. **Incorrect Answer A:** While tracing shapes can help with fine motor skills, it does not focus as much on the identification and description of shapes as the other activities. **Incorrect E**: Drawing pictures of shapes on the board and asking students to copy them into their notebooks primarily focuses on drawing skills rather than identifying and describing shapes in different contexts.
9.	D	Moving the decimal point one place to the left in the base ten system is equivalent to dividing by 10. For instance, moving the decimal point in 100.0 to the left results in 10.0, which is the same as dividing 100 by 10.
10.	D	**Correct Answer D:** Using paperclips to measure the length of students' desks provides a hands-on, concrete experience for young learners. This method helps them understand the concept of measurement and data collection in an engaging and developmentally appropriate way. **Incorrect Answer A:** While using a ruler to measure in inches is a valid activity, it may be too advanced for first graders who are just beginning to learn about measurement and data. **Incorrect Answer B:** Estimating with hands can be a fun activity but does not introduce students to the precision and recording aspects of measurement and data collection. **Incorrect Answer C:** Watching a video on measurement is informative but lacks the hands-on experience that is crucial for young learners to grasp measurement concepts effectively.

This page intentionally left blank.

VI. Constructed Response

The constructed response task for the Praxis 5024 Early Childhood Education exam requires test-takers to demonstrate their knowledge and application of teaching practices in early childhood settings. Examinees are given a scenario related to classroom instruction, student behavior, or curriculum planning and are asked to provide a detailed written response. The task involves:

1. **Analyzing the scenario:** Understand the specific needs or issues presented.

2. **Identifying strategies:** Propose effective, research-based strategies to address the scenario, including differentiation and appropriate educational practices.

3. **Providing justification:** Explain why these strategies are effective and how they support student learning and development.

The response should reflect a thorough understanding of early childhood education principles, including differentiated instruction, classroom management, and developmentally appropriate practices. The task assesses the ability to integrate theory into practical solutions for real-world classroom challenges.

This section of the study guide covers the following:

- Scoring Rubric
- Constructed Response 1 with sample response and discussion
- Constructed Response 2 with sample response and discussion
- Constructed Response 3 with sample response and discussion

Scoring Rubric

To meet the expectations in the provided rubric and achieve a passing score, test takers should ensure they address all parts of the question. Begin by carefully reading the question to understand its components, and then systematically address each part in your response.

Using specific words and phrases from the study guide can significantly enhance your writing, demonstrating familiarity with key concepts and pedagogical strategies. For example, incorporating terms like "Universal Design for Learning (UDL)," "least restrictive environment (LRE)," and "differentiated instruction" can showcase your understanding of essential educational principles.

Moreover, exhibiting a strong knowledge of students, subject matter, pedagogy, and relevant facts is crucial. To do this, provide specific examples and details in your explanations. For instance, if discussing strategies to support English Language Learners (ELLs), mention specific techniques such as using bilingual books, visual aids, and scaffolding. When referring to supporting students with IEPs, discuss accommodations like visual schedules and peer support systems.

Always aim to be as detailed as possible, illustrating your points with clear examples and evidence from the stimulus material or your own experience. Doing so demonstrates a thorough understanding and provides strong, detailed explanations that align with the rubric's criteria.

Generally, two readers grade your constructed responses. The highest score you can get for each question is a score of three from each reader, meaning there are six possible points for each question.

Below is the scoring criterion for each question. This rubric is simple. If you do these things in your writing, you will score well on this part of the exam.

Rubric - Score of 3

✓ Appropriately addresses all parts of the question.

✓ Shows a thorough understanding of any stimulus material presented.

✓ Exhibits a strong knowledge of students, subject matter, pedagogy, and/or facts relevant to the question.

✓ Provides strong explanations that are supported by details.

Quick Tip

The exam has three constructed-response questions, each graded by two readers. Each reader can give up to three points per question. This means each constructed-response question can earn a total of six points (three points from each reader). On your score report, you might see a score out of 18, representing the three questions (6 points each).

Here's an example:

- For the first question, one reader gives you a score of 2, and the other gives you a score of 3, for a total of 5 points.

- For the second question, you receive another 2 and 3 points from the readers, for a total of 5 points.

- For the third question, both readers give you a score of 2, for a total of 4 points.

When you add all these scores together, you get 14 out of 18 points for the constructed-response section.

Remember, the constructed response section is worth 20% of your overall test score. Therefore, it is important to practice your writing to ensure success on test day. The following are sample constructed response questions you can practice with. Also included are sample responses that meet the criteria of a score of three according to the rubric.

Constructed Response 1

Ms. Parker is a second-grade teacher with a diverse classroom of 25 students, including three special education students with Individualized Education Programs (IEPs) for speech-language services, a few English Language Learners (ELLs), and students with varied developmental needs.

As an early childhood educator, apply your knowledge of differentiated instruction, Universal Design for Learning (UDL), and holistic teaching approaches to address the needs of students with disabilities, ELLs, and others with various learning preferences. In your response:

1. Describe two specific strategies Ms. Parker could implement to ensure you are meeting the needs of all students.

2. Explain two methods Ms. Parker should use to create an inclusive and supportive learning environment for students with IEPs.

3. Detail how she could incorporate UDL principles and differentiated instruction to address the diverse needs, especially those who are ELL.

Example Response:

Ms. Parker can implement two strategies to ensure she is meeting the needs of all her students. First, she should use differentiated instruction to address the various learning preferences in her classroom. For instance, she can incorporate visual aids, hands-on activities, and auditory materials to cater to visual, kinesthetic, and auditory learners. Second, she can also use small-group instruction to provide targeted support and challenge students at their appropriate levels. By providing multiple means of representation, engagement, and expression, Ms. Parker can help all students access the curriculum and demonstrate their understanding in ways that suit their needs.

To create an inclusive and supportive learning environment for students with IEPs, Ms. Parker should first read the students' IEPs and determine what accommodations they need to thrive in her classroom. This will help ensure these students are placed in the least restrictive environment (LRE). Next, she can collaborate with special education teachers and speech-language pathologists to adapt lessons and provide accommodations, such as visual schedules, simplified instructions, and additional time for tasks. By promoting inclusivity and providing appropriate support, Ms. Parker can help her students with IEPs thrive academically and socially.

Incorporating Universal Design for Learning (UDL) principles and differentiated instruction is crucial in addressing the diverse needs of students, especially English Language Learners (ELLs). Ms. Parker should provide multiple means of representation by using bilingual books, visual aids, and multimedia resources to make content accessible for ELLs. She can also use scaffolding techniques, such as sentence starters and graphic organizers, to support language development and comprehension. For example, while some students might work on writing full sentences, others could match vocabulary words to pictures. Additionally, Ms. Parker should create opportunities for collaborative learning, where ELLs can practice language skills through peer interactions and group work. By incorporating UDL principles and differentiated instruction, Ms. Parker can ensure that all students receive the support they need to succeed regardless of their language proficiency.

Discussion:

There are several reasons why this response would get a score of three.

Rubric - Score of 3

- ✓ Appropriately addresses all parts of the question – Notice there are three paragraphs, one for each bullet in the task.

- ✓ Shows a thorough understanding of any stimulus material presented – Based on the response, it can be concluded that the test taker understood the scenario happening in the prompt.

- ✓ Exhibits a strong knowledge of students, subject matter, pedagogy, and/or facts relevant to the question – Notice throughout the response, the writer used specific vocabulary and examples that shows pedagogical knowledge.

- ✓ Provides strong explanations that are supported by details – in all three paragraphs, the writer uses phrases like *for example* and *for instance* to showcase specific examples to support the response.

Constructed Response 2

Ms. Morgan is a kindergarten teacher who has just administered an assessment on phonemic awareness and phonics to her students. Below is the classroom data set for eight students:

Student	Phonemic Awareness Score (out of 10)	Phonics Score (out of 10)
Alice	8	9
Ben	4	5
Carla	6	7
Daniel	3	4
Emily	9	10
Finn	5	6
Grace	7	8
Henry	2	3

Task:

1. Identify the areas of weakness for the students based on the provided data. Explain how Ms. Morgan can address these weaknesses with specific instructional strategies.

2. Describe how Ms. Morgan can use this data to make instructional decisions. Include at least one formative assessment to monitor progress and another assessment method to evaluate the effectiveness of instruction.

Example Response:

Based on the provided data, the areas of weakness for the students can be identified as follows: Ben, Daniel, and Henry are struggling in both phonemic awareness and phonics, with scores below 5 in both areas. These students require focused intervention to improve their skills in phonemic segmentation, blending, and letter-sound relationships.

To address these weaknesses, Ms. Morgan can implement several instructional strategies. First, for phonemic awareness, she could create small groups for targeted instruction, such as grouping Ben, Daniel, and Henry together to receive focused practice on phonemic segmentation and blending activities. Next, Ms. Morgan can incorporate a multi-sensory approach for phonics, using letter tiles for building words and phonics songs to reinforce letter-sound relationships. She could also provide decodable books that align with the phonics skills being taught, allowing students to apply their phonics knowledge in context, promoting reading fluency and confidence.

To ensure the strategies Ms. Morgan assigns are beneficial, she can first use diagnostic assessments to dig deeper into the specific skills the students are missing in phonemic awareness and phonics. These diagnostic assessments would help identify precise areas of difficulty, such as identifying beginning sounds, blending sounds, or recognizing letter-sound correspondences. She can also use ongoing formative assessments, such as observations with anecdotal notes on students' progress during phonemic awareness and phonics activities. Additionally, she can administer short, weekly phonics quizzes to monitor students' understanding and mastery of the skills taught. These quizzes would provide immediate feedback, allowing for timely instructional adjustments.

For summative assessment, she can use an end-of-unit test that includes phonemic awareness and phonics components to evaluate students' overall progress and the effectiveness of the instructional strategies. This comprehensive approach ensures that instructional decisions are data-driven and tailored to meet the individual needs of each student, promoting significant progress in their literacy development.

Discussion:

There are several reasons why this response would get a score of three.

Rubric - Score of 3

✓ Appropriately addresses all parts of the question – Notice the writer uses a paragraph for each element in the tasks: one paragraph to identify weaknesses, another paragraph to discuss applicable strategies, another for formative assessments, and another for summative assessments. This helps to keep ideas organized and makes it easy for the reader to see that you have satisfied all areas of the question.

✓ Shows a thorough understanding of any stimulus material presented – Based on the response, it can be concluded that the test taker understood the data presented in the prompt.

✓ Exhibits a strong knowledge of students, subject matter, pedagogy, and/or facts relevant to the question – Notice throughout the response, the writer used specific vocabulary and examples that shows pedagogical knowledge.

✓ Provides strong explanations that are supported by details – in all three paragraphs, the writer uses phrases like *for example* and *for instance* to showcase specific examples to support the response. Specific strategies and types of assessments are mentioned.

Constructed Response 3

Ms. Brown is a first-grade teacher who is preparing her classroom environment to support her students' learning goals. In her diverse classroom, Ms. Brown has students with various abilities and needs, including English Language Learners (ELLs) and students with disabilities who have Individualized Education Programs (IEPs) for speech and language delays. Some students need additional math support, while others have advanced reading skills. She also has students with sensory processing needs and those who benefit from structured routines due to attention difficulties. Considering these varied needs, Ms. Brown plans to create an inclusive and supportive learning environment for all her students.

Task:

1. Describe how Ms. Brown can organize the physical configuration of her classroom to support her learning goals.

2. Explain how Ms. Brown can ensure students are maximizing learning time while also enjoying a structured, safe learning environment.

3. Discuss how Ms. Brown can match different learning configurations to the needs of her students as individuals and as part of a group.

Example Response

To support her learning goals, Ms. Brown can organize the physical configuration of her classroom by creating distinct learning centers. These centers will be designed to target specific skills and subjects, such as a reading center, a math center, a science exploration area, and an art station. Each center will have relevant materials and resources, such as books, manipulatives, and art supplies, to facilitate hands-on learning. Additionally, Ms. Brown should ensure that the centers are clearly labeled and easily accessible, allowing students to navigate and utilize the spaces independently. Flexible seating options, such as floor cushions and small tables, can also be incorporated to accommodate various learning styles and preferences. This arrangement promotes student engagement and allows for differentiated instruction. She could include a sensory corner with tools like fidget toys and noise-canceling headphones for students with sensory processing needs to help them stay focused and calm.

To ensure students are maximizing learning while in a safe and secure learning environment, Ms. Brown can create practice routines and procedures for her classroom. She can create a daily schedule that balances whole group instruction, small group activities, and individual work time. She can then model and practice these routines with students. The schedule should be posted prominently in the classroom and reviewed with students each morning to set daily expectations. For example, Ms. Brown can implement a visual schedule with pictures and words to help students understand and follow the daily routine. Regularly scheduled times for centers, group work, and independent reading can provide stability and help students develop self-regulation skills. She can schedule extra practice time during the day for students who require additional math support.

Ms. Brown can use various instructional strategies to match different learning configurations to the needs of her students. For whole-group instruction, she can introduce new concepts and conduct read-alouds, ensuring all students receive the same information. Small group activities, such as guided reading groups or math problem-solving teams, can provide targeted instruction based on students' skill levels. Pairing students for peer tutoring or collaborative projects can foster social skills and reinforce learning through peer interactions. One-on-one configurations are essential for individualized support, such as providing additional help to students who need more intensive instruction. Learning centers allow students to work independently or in small groups, promoting autonomy and active engagement. By using a mix of these configurations, Ms. Brown can address the diverse needs of her students and create a dynamic and inclusive classroom environment. For her ELL students, she can incorporate language-rich activities and peer interactions to enhance their language development, while students with IEPs can receive tailored support in the least restrictive environment (LRE).

Discussion:

There are several reasons why this response would get a score of three.

Rubric - Score of 3

- ✓ Appropriately addresses all parts of the question – Notice the writer uses a paragraph for each element in the tasks. This helps to keep ideas organized and makes it easy for the reader to see that you have satisfied all areas of the question.

- ✓ Shows a thorough understanding of any stimulus material presented – Based on the response, it can be concluded that the test taker understood the scenario presented in the prompt.

- ✓ Exhibits a strong knowledge of students, subject matter, pedagogy, and/or facts relevant to the question – Notice throughout the response, the writer used specific vocabulary and examples that shows pedagogical knowledge.

- ✓ Provides strong explanations that are supported by details – in all three paragraphs, the writer uses phrases like *for example* and *for instance* to showcase specific examples to support the response. Specific strategies and types of assessments are mentioned.

1. How can a teacher modify a painting activity to accommodate the physical development differences between a 3-year-old and an 8-year-old child?

   A. Provide thicker brushes and larger paper for the 3-year-old; offer fine brushes and detailed canvases for the 8-year-old.

   B. Give both age groups the same materials to encourage creativity.

   C. Focus on finger painting for the 8-year-old and watercolor for the 3-year-old.

   D. Avoid painting activities for the 3-year-old and focus on drawing for the 8-year-old.

2. How can a teacher adapt a climbing activity for a 3-year-old child compared to an 8-year-old child to match their physical development levels?

   A. Use a low, soft climbing structure for the 3-year-old; use a more complex and higher climbing apparatus for the 8-year-old

   B. Use the same climbing structure for both age groups to ensure equality.

   C. Avoid climbing activities for the 3-year-old and focus on running activities for the 8-year-old.

   D. Use video simulations of climbing for both age groups.

3. Which of the following activities would be appropriate for assessing the fine motor development of a 4-year-old child?

   A. Ask the child to write their name on lined paper.

   B. Encourage the child to balance on one foot.

   C. Require the child to draw intricate designs

   D. Have the child use scissors to cut out simple shapes.

4. What is within the typical range of gross motor development for a 4-year-old child?

   A. Tying shoelaces independently

   B. Writing complete sentences

   C. Playing a musical instrument proficiently

   D. Dancing to music during

5. How might a 6-year-old child solve a puzzle differently than an 8-year-old?

   A. A 6-year-old might use trial and error, while an 8-year-old might use more systematic approaches.

   B. Both age groups will use the same strategies.

   C. The 6-year-old will avoid puzzles, while the 8-year-old will solve them instantly.

   D. The 8-year-old will solve puzzles without difficulty, while the 6-year-old will struggle.

6. What is a significant difference in the problem-solving strategies of a 6-year-old compared to an 8-year-old?

    A. A 6-year-old will seek help immediately, while an 8-year-old will refuse help.

    B. Both age groups will depend entirely on adult guidance.

    C. A 6-year-old will likely experiment more, while an 8-year-old will plan and strategize.

    D. A 6-year-old will understand abstract concepts, while an 8-year-old will not.

7. Which of the following statements best describes how environment and inheritance shape cognitive ability?

    A. Genetic inheritance is the primary factor, with some influence from the environment.

    B. Environmental factors play a crucial role and are often more impactful than genetics.

    C. Both genetic inheritance and environmental factors interact dynamically to shape cognitive ability.

    D. Cognitive ability is fixed at birth and cannot be altered by environmental factors.

8. Ms. Hernandez wants to create a learning environment that is healthy, respectful, supportive, and challenging for her first-grade students. Which strategies best demonstrate her application of developmental knowledge to achieve this goal? Choose **ALL** that apply.

    ☐ A. Implement a strict discipline system to maintain order.

    ☐ B. Provide a variety of learning activities at different developmental stages.

    ☐ C. Allow students to complete all tasks independently without teacher intervention.

    ☐ D. Focus on academic achievement to maintain equity.

    ☐ E. Practice routines and procedures to maximize learning.

9. Ms. Thompson, a first-grade teacher, notices that one of her students, Liam, often comes to school without breakfast and seems tired and distracted.

How might Liam's nutrition and health impact his physical, cognitive, and emotional development, and what could Ms. Thompson do to support him?

    A. Liam's nutrition and health likely have no impact on his development; therefore, Ms. Thompson should focus solely on academic interventions.

    B. Poor nutrition and health are only related to physical development; therefore, cognitive and emotional development remain unaffected.

    C. Proper nutrition must start at home; Ms. Thompson should notify the parents and ensure they provide Liam with enough food.

    D. Poor nutrition and health can significantly impact a child's physical energy; therefore, Ms. Thompson should ensure Liam has access to the school's breakfast program.

10. Mr. Kim is preparing for a new school year and wants to better understand his students' diverse family and community backgrounds to support their learning. How can he be informed of these characteristics without violating the privacy of individual families?

    A. Send out a detailed survey asking for personal family information.

    B. Hold a class meeting to discuss each student's family background publicly.

    C. Use general information from parent-teacher conferences, community events, and school records to gain insights while respecting privacy.

    D. Request access to confidential family records from the school administration.

11. Ms. Patel has a student, Arjun, whose family speaks primarily Hindi at home. She wants to ensure that her teaching methods are inclusive and supportive of Arjun's linguistic background.

    How can Ms. Patel support Arjun's learning while being sensitive to his home language and culture?

    A. Ignore Arjun's home language and focus solely on English to avoid confusion.

    B. Expect Arjun to translate for his peers to enhance his English skills.

    C. Avoid involving Arjun's family in his education to respect their privacy.

    D. Incorporate bilingual resources and communicate with the family to better understand Arjun's linguistic needs.

12. Mr. Bennett notices that one of his third-grade students, Sarah, often appears tired and hungry when she arrives at school. She struggles to concentrate in class and frequently falls asleep at her desk.

    According to Maslow's hierarchy of needs, which level of needs should Mr. Bennett address first to help Sarah improve her concentration and engagement in class?

    A. Esteem Needs

    B. Self-Actualization Needs

    C. Safety Needs

    D. Physiological Needs

13. Ms. Roberts is developing a classroom environment that aims to support her students' diverse needs. She wants to ensure that her students feel safe and secure in her classroom before focusing on their academic achievements and self-esteem.

    Which of the following strategies aligns with addressing safety needs in Maslow's hierarchy of needs?

    A. Encouraging students to participate in group projects to build a sense of belonging.

    B. Providing a consistent classroom routine and clear rules to create a stable environment.

    C. Praising students for their academic achievements to boost their confidence.

    D. Offering opportunities for creative expression through art and music.

14. Ms. Jackson is a preschool teacher who has been informed that one of her students, Tommy, has recently been diagnosed with a speech delay and now has an IEP in place.

    Which of the following actions should Ms. Jackson take to ensure she effectively supports Tommy's IEP goals?

    A. Create a separate curriculum for Tommy that is different from the rest of the class.

    B. Collaborate with the speech therapist to incorporate recommended activities into Tommy's daily routine.

    C. Allow Tommy to skip speech activities to focus more on other academic areas.

    D. Expect Tommy to follow the same activities as the other students without modifications.

15. Mr. Lopez is preparing for an upcoming IEP meeting for his student, Emily, who has a learning disability. He wants to ensure that he provides valuable input and effectively participates in the meeting.

    What is one important step Mr. Lopez should take to prepare for Emily's IEP meeting?

    A. Review Emily's current performance data and prepare to discuss her progress and areas of need.

    B. Create a new set of goals for Emily before consulting other team members.

    C. Focus on Emily's behavior in the classroom more than her academic performance.

    D. Plan to discuss only the positive aspects of Emily's performance to avoid conflict.

16. Which of the following lists all the concepts of number sense that a child at the preoperational stage can typically understand?

    A. Counting up to 10

    B. Counting up to 10 and recognizing basic shapes

    C. Counting up to 10, recognizing basic shapes, and understanding one-to-one correspondence

    D. Counting up to 10, recognizing basic shapes, understanding one-to-one correspondence, and performing multiplication

17. Ms. Carter is a first-grade teacher who has three students with Individualized Education Programs (IEPs) requiring occupational therapy services. These services are scheduled during the class's art time, but Ms. Carter often keeps the students in class for art because she believes it enhances their creativity. Which of the following best explains why Ms. Carter is in violation of the students' IEPs?

    A. Ms. Carter is not allowing the students to participate in the least restrictive environment.

    B. Ms. Carter's actions result in the occupational therapist being paid for services that are not being delivered.

    C. Ms. Carter is providing additional creative activities that are not included in the students' IEPs.

    D. Ms. Carter is not ensuring the specific supports outlined in the students' IEPs are being provided.

18. Sam is five years old in a preschool class. His teacher and the school psychologist recommend that Sam wait one more year before entering kindergarten. These educators feel that this would give Sam more time to develop and become ready for kindergarten. Which of the following theories does this assertion align with?

    A. Psychoanalytic theory

    B. Maturational theory

    C. Sociocultural theory

    D. Behavioral theory

19. The following are observations made by a teacher about several 8-year-old children's academic and behavioral behaviors:

    • Alex sometimes struggles to complete two-step math problems and frequently asks for help.

    • Mia sometimes disrupts the class by talking out of turn and interrupting others.

    • Ethan brags about his achievements in science and pretends not to need help, even when he does.

    • Olivia consistently fails to turn in homework and appears unable to follow sequences in instructions.

    Based on these observations, which child's academic and behavioral development should the teacher be most concerned about?

    A. Alex

    B. Mia

    C. Ethan

    D. Olivia

20. Mrs. Green is teaching a second-grade class about buoyancy using a constructivist approach. She gives the students various objects to place in water to see which float and sink. The students observe that some heavy objects float while some light objects sink. Which of the following teacher actions would best help the students understand the principles of buoyancy?

   A. Explaining to the students that an object's buoyancy is related to its density compared to the density of water

   B. Showing a video that explains how the shape of an object can affect its ability to float

   C. Encouraging students to test more objects and make predictions to understand why some objects float and others sink

   D. Asking students to draw pictures of floating objects and write about them in their journals

21. Which of the following is the best example of how a kindergarten teacher can foster a supportive and inclusive classroom environment for young children?

   A. Organize the classroom furniture to create clear pathways and reduce physical hazards.

   B. Teach children to celebrate and appreciate each other's cultural backgrounds.

   C. Provide a variety of art supplies for creative expression during free play.

   D. Create a visual schedule to help children understand the daily routine.

22. Which of the following is the best example of a child demonstrating characteristics typical of Piaget's preoperational stage of cognitive development?

   A. Jamie experiments with objects by throwing them to see what happens.

   B. Alex understands that other children may have different perspectives and opinions.

   C. Emma creates imaginary scenarios and roles during playtime

   D. Ryan uses logical thinking to solve puzzles systematically.

23. Ms. Thompson is preparing a lesson on addition for her second-grade class, which includes students with varying abilities and learning styles. To ensure she is providing the most effective instruction, which of the following strategies should she use to cater to the diverse needs of her students?

   A. Give all students the same worksheet with identical addition problems to complete independently.

   B. Set up differentiated learning centers with various addition activities tailored to different ability levels and learning styles.

   C. Deliver a lecture on addition principles and allow time for students to ask specific questions.

   D. Focus on advanced students, providing them with challenging problems while letting other students practice basic skills independently.

24. Mr. Rivera is designing a reading lesson for his first-grade class, which includes students with a wide range of developmental differences. To ensure he is applying Universal Design for Learning (UDL) principles, which of the following strategies should he use to make the lesson accessible and beneficial for all students?

   A. Offer multiple means of representation, such as audiobooks, visual aids, and interactive e-books, to present the reading material.

   B. Provide a single reading passage for all students to read independently.

   C. Deliver a lecture on the reading material and expect all students to take notes and answer questions.

   D. Focus on students with advanced reading skills and give them additional challenging texts while others work on the standard passage.

25. Ms. Lee is planning her curriculum for a diverse kindergarten class. She wants to adopt a holistic approach to teaching that addresses students' cognitive, social, emotional, physical, and language needs. Which of the following strategies best aligns with a holistic approach?

A. Focusing on academic skills such as reading and math during classroom time.

B. Integrating activities that promote movement, journal writing, role play, and speaking into the daily schedule.

C. Using standardized tests and essay assignments to measure student progress and development.

D. Assigning independent study projects that students can design themselves and complete at their own pace.

26. A teacher has observed a child and writes a summary of her observations. Which of the following summaries represents an interference rather than an objective statement of behavior?

A. John played with blocks for ten minutes, building a tower and then knocking it down repeatedly.

B. Lisa looked at the clock several times during the math lesson and fidgeted in her seat.

C. Kevin smiled and laughed while playing tag with his friends on the playground.

D. Sarah's behavior of sitting quietly in the corner and avoiding eye contact suggests she feels lonely and isolated.

27. After the universal screening process and an oral reading analysis using grade-level text, three second-grade students in Ms. Jefferson's class have been identified as at risk. What should Ms. Jefferson do next in helping these at-risk students?

A. Administer a series of diagnostic assessments focused on specific skills such as phonemic awareness, phonics, word recognition.

B. Provide opportunities for the students to engage in choral reading to become comfortable with reading aloud and building fluency.

C. Group the at-risk students together and provide them with low-level text so they can practice their reading.

D. Request that a specialist come pull students out of class and work with them individually to help them increase their skills.

28. Which of the following is the most effective way to use assessments in the reading classroom?

A. To determine students' reading comprehension

B. To determine students' vocabulary acquisition.

C. To determine students' phonics skill levels.

D. To make instructional decisions.

29. A teacher is planning to implement evidence-based reading strategies in the classroom and wants to determine whether these strategies are effective for her students. What assessments should the teacher use to measure this?

   A. Start with a universal screening test, then a summative assessment mid-semester, then a norm-referenced assessment at the end of the semester.

   B. Use a diagnostic pretest at the beginning of the semester, formative assessments throughout the semester, and then a summative at the end of the semester.

   C. Administer a norm-referenced exam to compare students at the beginning of the semester, followed by a criterion-referenced assessment at the end of the semester.

   D. Give students formative assessments throughout the semester and a universal screening test to determine students' levels.

30. Ms. Anderson is assessing her preschool students' literacy development using both qualitative and quantitative data. Which of the following scenarios best demonstrates her effective use of both types of data to inform her instruction?

   A. Ms. Anderson administers a standardized literacy test to all students and uses the scores to group them by ability.

   B. Ms. Anderson takes detailed observational notes on each child's reading behavior and creates individual reading profiles based on her notes.

   C. Ms. Anderson uses a checklist to count the number of sight words each child can recognize and maintains anecdotal records of their engagement and strategies during reading activities.

   D. Ms. Anderson relies on anecdotal records and informal conversations with the children to assess their literacy skills.

31. Ms. Turner wants to collect comprehensive data on her students' development in a structured and consistent manner. Which combination of methods would best help her achieve this goal?

   A. Use systematic observations with structured protocols, maintain checklists and rubrics, and compile student portfolios.

   B. Conduct diagnostic assessments and informal observations to discuss findings with colleagues.

   C. Rely on state standardized criterion-referenced and norm-referenced test scores to assess students' progress.

   D. Keep anecdotal records and review student work with colleagues and parents.

32. Which type of assessment is best described by ongoing evaluations that monitor student learning and provide feedback for instructional adjustments, often using methods such as observations and daily quizzes?

   A. Summative

   B. Criterion-Referenced

   C. Norm-Referenced

   D. Formative

33. Ms. Johnson wants to assess her third-grade students' understanding of the state's mathematics standards. She decides to use a specific type of assessment that measures each student's performance against the established state standards. Which of the following assessment methods should Ms. Johnson use?

    A. Norm-Referenced Assessment

    B. Criterion-Referenced Assessment

    C. Formative Assessment

    D. Performance-Based Assessment

34. Which type of assessment involves students demonstrating their knowledge and skills through practical tasks such as science experiments, presentations, and art projects?

    A. Formative

    B. Summative

    C. Performance-Based

    D. Portfolio

35. Ms. Carter uses anecdotal records to assess her kindergarten students' progress. Which of the following best explains how anecdotal records can be used to demonstrate what a student can do?

    A. Anecdotal records provide a quantitative measure of a student's skills through test scores.

    B. Anecdotal records offer a detailed, narrative description of a student's behaviors and skills in various situations.

    C. Anecdotal records include standardized test results that compare the student to a norm group.

    D. Anecdotal records summarize the student's performance on multiple-choice exams.

36. Ms. Johnson, a preschool teacher, plans to introduce her four-year-old students to the formal symbols for the numbers one through ten. Which of the following methods would be the most appropriate way to assess if the children are ready for this learning task?

    A. Ask the children to count out loud up to ten.

    B. Have the children sort various objects based on their shapes.

    C. Encourage the children to create groups of two and three objects.

    D. Observe the children as they engage in on-to-one correspondence.

37. What is the role of the teacher in the process of referring a child for speech services?

    A. Identify signs of potential speech difficulties, document observations, and communicate with parents and speech-language pathologists to initiate the referral process.

    B. Diagnose the child with a speech disorder, prescribe specific therapies, and communicate next steps with parents.

    C. Conduct formal speech therapy sessions with the child in the classroom and encourage parents do the same at home.

    D. Wait for the parents to notice the speech issue and request an evaluation from the school.

38. What is the primary purpose of creating a multidimensional assessment for students with cultural and linguistic differences?

   A. To provide a comprehensive evaluation that considers students' diverse backgrounds and identifies their unique strengths and needs.

   B. To compare students' performance to a standard norm group so their cultural and linguistic abilities do not impede their progression.

   C. To simplify the assessment process by using a single method for all students, ensuring equity and equality.

   D. To ensure that all students are evaluated based on their English language proficiency and not by their any specific culture.

39. Mr. Davis wants to evaluate the social interactions and academic progress of his kindergarten students. Which of the following methods would best allow him to gather both qualitative and quantitative data?

   A. Conducting one-on-one interviews with students about their favorite activities and documenting their responses.

   B. Use a rating scale to measure students' ability to share and cooperate during group activities and maintain a journal of specific incidents where students demonstrate these skills.

   C. Give a math skills test and rank students based on their scores.

   D. Create a visual chart to track daily attendance and award stars for perfect attendance.

40. Ms. Lee uses anecdotal records to assess her preschool students' early math skills. Which anecdotal notes provide the most relevant data for determining a student's understanding of number sense and counting?

   A. "During center time, Jake sorted blocks by color and shape, making separate piles for each category."

   B. "During snack time, Maria counted out ten crackers for herself and ten for her friend, ensuring they each had the same amount."

   C. "During playtime, Sam measured the length of the classroom rug using a tape measure and reported the number of inches."

   D. "During art class, Olivia identified shapes like circles, squares, and triangles in her drawing and described them."

41. Ms. Nguyen evaluates her kindergarten students using various assessment methods. For math skills, she decides to use a performance-based assessment. Which of the following best describes an advantage of using performance-based assessments in math?

   A. They provide a quick and efficient way to measure students' knowledge through multiple-choice questions.

   B. They offer a standardized comparison of students' abilities against national benchmarks.

   C. Rather than standard algorithms, they rely on word problems, which are more effective in seeing student progress.

   D. They allow students to demonstrate their skills and knowledge through practical tasks, providing a more comprehensive view of their abilities.

42. Which of the following statements best describes a disadvantage of using standardized tests in early childhood education?

    A. They provide inconsistent and unreliable data that cannot be compared across different populations.

    B. They lack details and insights into individual students' critical thinking abilities.

    C. They may not accurately reflect the abilities of students with cultural and linguistic differences, leading to potential biases in results.

    D. They require long periods of time before assessment data can be evaluated and used.

43. Indicate **FOUR** ways in which assessment results can be communicated to families effectively.

    ☐ A. Provide written reports with detailed explanations of assessment results and suggested activities for home support.

    ☐ B. Share pieces of the data that parents can understand, leaving out the more complicated figures needed only for educators.

    ☐ C. Hold face-to-face meetings or conferences to discuss assessment results and answer any questions the parents might have.

    ☐ D. Provide visual aids, such as charts and graphs, to help explain the assessment results clearly.

    ☐ E. Offer workshops or informational sessions for parents to understand how to interpret assessment results and use them to support their child's learning.

44. Mr. Martinez wants to ensure the accuracy of his students' assessment results by using triangulation. Which of the following methods best demonstrates triangulation in the assessment process?

    A. Rely on standardized test scores to evaluate three types of student performance.

    B. Combine observations, student work samples, and standardized test scores to confirm findings.

    C. Use anecdotal records collected over the school year to assess student progress in three areas of behavior.

    D. Administer multiple-choice quizzes periodically and average the scores for final grades.

45. Ms. Anderson is designing her classroom to accommodate students with physical and emotional disabilities, ensuring she adheres to least restrictive environment (LRE) principles. Which of the following plans best aligns with LRE principles while meeting the needs of all students?

    A. Create a separate classroom area for students with disabilities, ensuring they have specialized equipment and resources away from their peers.

    B. Integrate students with disabilities into the general classroom, providing necessary accommodations such as assistive technology.

    C. Place students with disabilities in the general classroom without additional supports, to promote independence and equal treatment.

    D. Assign a dedicated aide to each student with a disability and follow the accommodations in the IEP.

46. Ms. Carter is preparing to read a book about frogs to her kindergarten class and wants to gauge the students' existing knowledge on the topic. Which of the following strategies would be most effective for this purpose?

    A. Incorporate information about frogs into different subjects throughout the week.

    B. Demonstrate directionality by reading about frogs in a big book in the front of class.

    C. Encourage students to look at and discuss the pictures in the book before reading.

    D. Present developmentally appropriate scientific facts about frogs before reading.

47. Ms. Rodriguez is an early childhood teacher with three students with IEPs in her class. Two students are supposed to receive services with an occupational therapist during the school day. Ms. Rodriguez does not send the students down to occupational therapy and instead keeps them in their reading block. She believes the reading block is more important than occupational therapy. Is Ms. Rodriguez in violation of the students' IEPs, and why?

A. Yes, an IEP is a legal document, and all accommodations in it must be followed under federal law.

B. Yes, Ms. Rodriguez is discriminating against these students by failing to provide the least restrictive environment.

C. No, Ms. Rodriguez has the authority as the teacher to ensure her students receive adequate reading instruction.

D. No, Ms. Rodriguez can keep the students in class if she has permission from the occupational therapist.

48. As part of a science unit on plant growth, Ms. Thompson invites a local gardener to her kindergarten class. Which of the following would be the most effective use of the gardener as an outside resource?

A. Have the gardener talk about the benefits of a gardening career.

B. Ask the gardener to distribute seeds and plant pots to each child.

C. Have the gardener demonstrate how to plant seeds and care for them, allowing the children to practice planting.

D. Have the gardener show pictures of neglected plants and discuss the importance of plant care.

49. Ms. Turner is setting up a fish tank in her kindergarten classroom to teach her students about aquatic life and responsibility through observing and caring for the fish. Which of the following strategies would best set her students up for success in this area using developmentally appropriate practices? Choose **ALL** that apply.

☐ A. Placing the fish tank next to the computer and listening stations, where students can listen to instructions while observing the fish.

☐ B. Setting a rotating schedule for students to feed the fish, clean the tank, and record observations, ensuring each child has a turn and understands their responsibilities.

☐ C. Allowing only a few selected students to care for the fish to ensure proper maintenance and reduce the risk of mistakes.

☐ D. Demonstrating how to care for the fish with detailed step-by-step, explicit instructions.

☐ E. Establishing a routine for feeding and caring for the fish, making it part of the daily classroom schedule.

☐ F. Placing the fish tank in a corner of the room to avoid distractions and minimize interaction during core academics.

50. Ms. Patel is planning a math activity for her prekindergarten class to help students understand the concepts of "put together" and "take away". Which of the following activities would best achieve this objective?

A. Give students worksheets with addition and subtraction problems to complete independently.

B. Use counting bears to show how adding or taking bears away from a group changes the total number.

C. Show a video about basic addition and subtraction concepts and ask students to discuss them afterward.

D. Read a story about numbers and ask students to draw pictures of the story's events.

51. Ms. Taylor, a prekindergarten teacher, notices that when she places pictures of different types of animals in the art center, the children's drawings and sculptures become more detailed. Which of the following questions could she ask the children to help them apply principles of observation and creativity to their work?

A. How many colors did you use in your drawing?

B. What materials did you use most often in your sculpture?

C. How could you make your sculpture more realistic?

D. How is your drawing different from the animal in the picture?

52. Ms. Lawson is working with her kindergarten students on recognizing and continuing patterns using shape tiles. One student has placed two shapes in a sequence that does not match the established pattern. Which of the following questions or statements would be most appropriate for the teacher to pose at this point?

A. "That is incorrect. Please try again?"

B. "Can you tell me why you chose those two shapes?"

C. "There are three parts to the design. Do you see them?"

D. "Watch me as I demonstrate the design."

53. While working with two-year-old Max, a teacher observes that Max says, "Want juice" when he probably means, "I want some juice." Which of the following responses by the teacher would be most appropriate?

A. Take no special action since Max's wording is age appropriate.

B. Correct Max immediately and ask him to repeat the sentence correctly.

C. Create a series of lessons on sentence structure for the entire class.

D. Discuss Max's speech development with his parents during a conference and suggest natural correction at home.

54. Which of the following groups of objects would be the best selection to aid four-year-old children in developing initial concepts about the physical characteristics of different objects?

A. Toy fruits, pictures of fruits, stories about fruits, and a fruit-scented air freshener

B. A variety of leaves, pictures of trees, stories about forests, and a recording of birds chirping

C. Plastic cups, metal spoons, rubber bands, and glass marbles

D. Feathers, cotton balls, smooth stones, and rough sandpaper

55. Ms. Simmons is arranging her first-grade classroom to accommodate a vision-impaired student. Which of the following strategies would best support this student's learning needs?

A. Place the student at the back of the classroom with a paraprofessional to aid the student and minimize distractions.

B. Position the student near the windows to utilize natural light and provide standard-sized textbooks and handouts in Braille.

C. Seat the student in the middle of the classroom to allow easy interaction with peers and provide auditory learning aids.

D. Seat the student close to the front of the classroom where they have an unobstructed view of the teacher and instructional materials.

56. Ms. Martinez is planning a math lesson using the gradual release of responsibility model to scaffold learning. Which of the following sequences best illustrates this model?

   A. Allow students to practice independently first, then engage them in guided practice, and conclude with direct instruction.

   B. Begin with direct instruction, move to guided practice, and then allow students to practice independently.

   C. Engage students in group work, then have them work independently, followed by direct instruction.

   D. Start with independent practice, provide additional resources, and end with whole-group instruction.

57. Mr. Johnson wants to tailor his reading instruction to meet the individual needs of his students. Which of the following strategies best demonstrates differentiation?

   A. Use flexible grouping, offering choice in assignments, and providing additional resources for advanced learners or extra support for those who need it.

   B. Provide differentiated reading assignments to all students and offer extra help during recess for those who need it.

   C. Assign challenging books to advanced readers and easier books to struggling readers, slightly modifying the instructional approach.

   D. Use whole-group instruction and periodically check for understanding through quizzes.

58. Ms. Green wants to encourage critical-thinking skills in her third-grade class by using questioning techniques. Which of the following questions would best achieve this goal?

   A. Why does the caterpillar turn into a butterfly?

   B. Using the map, can you identify the continent of Africa?

   C. Can you name all the planets in our solar system?

   D. How many sides does a hexagon have?

59. Mr. Thompson wants to use problem-based learning (PBL) to engage his third-grade students in critical thinking in math. Which of the following activities best exemplifies PBL?

   A. Assign a worksheet with complex word problems to be completed in pairs.

   B. Have students memorize and recite math addition facts using numbers 1-10.

   C. Assign a multiple-choice quiz on concepts the class reviewed earlier in the week.

   D. Have students apply their addition and subtraction skills to a simple budget.

60. Ms. Rivera wants to encourage her second-grade students to explore and experiment to develop their critical thinking skills. Which of the following activities would be most effective?

   A. Read a chapter from a science textbook and discuss the vocabulary with partners.

   B. Watch a documentary about space and answer complex questions about the video.

   C. Conduct an experiment to see which type of soil best supports plant growth.

   D. Read a paragraph about cell structures in cooperative groups and take notes.

61. Ms. Carter is implementing a blended learning approach in her third-grade classroom. Which of the following strategies best exemplifies blended learning?

   A. Use textbooks and classroom lectures to teach core academic subjects and artificial intelligence to teach the arts.

   B. Assign students online modules to complete independently at home that accompany direct instruction in the classroom.

   C. Combine classroom lectures with online assignments that students can complete at their own pace, allowing personalized learning experiences.

   D. Explore artificial intelligence and document-sharing software to enhance students' writing experiences and teach them to avoid plagiarism.

62. Ms. Lopez wants to establish routines in her kindergarten classroom to help children develop self-regulation and independence. Which of the following strategies best accomplishes this goal?

   A. Establish clear routines for arrival and departure, transitioning between activities and clean-up times, with visual aids and sequences to support understanding.

   B. Allow students to choose the classroom expectations, promoting flexibility and compliance.

   C. Encourage students to follow classroom expectations by implementing a system of rewards and consequences.

   D. Use a predictable schedule daily to keep students on task and provide consequences for those who do not comply.

63. Mr. Parker wants a classroom environment that accommodates various planned activities. Which of the following strategies would best achieve this goal?

   A. Arrange fixed furniture in a traditional classroom layout with rows of desks facing the teacher so students can easily transition to activities throughout the day.

   B. Use flexible spaces where children can engage in specific types of activities.

   C. Set up stations for each subject area to ensure students always know where to go.

   D. Keep the classroom layout static to minimize disruptions and maintain order.

64. Mr. Thompson has a student with a mild hearing impairment in his second-grade class. Which of the following strategies best aligns with the concept of least restrictive environment (LRE)?

   A. Assign the student to a special education classroom full-time to ensure they receive specialized instruction.

   B. Provide the student with assistive listening devices following the IEP and seat them near the front of the class.

   C. Have the student attend general education classes for art and physical education while receiving all core instruction in a special education setting.

   D. Exempt the student from participating in group activities to minimize their frustration.

65. Ms. Johnson, a second-grade teacher, has been keeping detailed records of her students' progress and behavior. She wants to share these records with a parent volunteer who helps with classroom activities. According to the Family Educational Rights and Privacy Act (FERPA), what should Ms. Johnson do?

   A. Share the records with the parent volunteer to keep them informed and engaged in the classroom.

   B. Share the records with the parent volunteer only after obtaining written consent from the students' parents.

   C. Discuss the students' progress and behavior data with the parent volunteer during parent-teacher conferences.

   D. Use the records to inform her teaching but keep them confidential and not share them with the parent volunteer.

66. Ms. Collins is part of a school-based professional learning community (PLC) at her elementary school. Which of the following activities would best exemplify the purpose of a PLC?

   A. Meet once a month to plan the school's social events and extracurricular activities.

   B. Discuss student progress, share effective teaching strategies, and analyze classroom data to improve instruction.

   C. Hold occasional workshops to learn about the latest educational technology tools without implementing them.

   D. Gather to discuss school policy changes and administrative issues.

67. Ms. Thompson, an early childhood educator, is concerned about one of her students, Emily, who has been struggling with reading comprehension. How would conferring with colleagues and paraprofessionals help Ms. Thompson better understand Emily's needs?

   A. It helps Ms. Thompson gather diverse perspectives and strategies from other educators who may have observed similar challenges in different contexts.

   B. It allows Ms. Thompson to receive administrative support for classroom management issues.

   C. It provides Ms. Thompson with the opportunity to transfer Emily to a different class with a different teacher.

   D. It enables Ms. Thompson to delegate her teaching responsibilities to paraprofessionals while focusing on other students.

68. Ms. Rivera, a kindergarten teacher, wants to improve her teaching practices and the learning environment in her classroom. Which self-assessment techniques would best help her reflect on her practices?

   A. Keep a detailed reflective journal to document her daily teaching experiences and student interactions.

   B. Ask her students to complete a survey about their favorite classroom activities and how they feel about instruction.

   C. Use end-of-year student test scores to evaluate her teaching effectiveness.

   D. Observe other teachers' classrooms to compare her teaching style with theirs.

69. A kindergarten teacher notices that one of her students, Lucas, has significant delays in his ability to run, jump, and balance. Which of the following describes his issues and the most suitable professional to help him?

    A. Fine motor skills - Occupational therapist

    B. Fine motor skills - Speech therapist

    C. Gross motor skills - Physical therapist

    D. Gross motor skills - Paraprofessional

70. What would be the most appropriate communication technology for a kindergarten teacher to use when communicating with parents?

    A. Word processing software to create newsletters.

    B. Virtual parent-teacher conferences.

    C. Class website, email updates, and a mobile app

    D. YouTube, social media, and blogs.

71. Ms. Walker, a first-grade teacher, wants to understand how her students' learning might be affected by their family and community characteristics, such as family structure, socioeconomic conditions, home language, ethnicity, religion, culture, and any stresses or supports. Which of the following methods would best inform her of these characteristics without violating the privacy of individual families? Choose **ALL** that apply.

    ☐ A. Distribute surveys to gather general information about family and community characteristics.

    ☐ B. Observe students' behavior and interactions in the classroom.

    ☐ C. Have students write essays about their home lives and family situations.

    ☐ D. Collaborate with school counselors and other professionals who can provide relevant insights.

    ☐ E. Review cumulative records and reports that include background information shared by previous teachers.

    ☐ F. Hold regular parent-teacher conferences to discuss each child's background and needs.

72. Ms. Anderson, a preschool teacher, wants to design an activity that creates a welcoming environment and promotes family involvement and partnerships. Which of the following activities would best achieve this goal?

    A. Organize a classroom open house where students present their artwork and projects to family members and guardians.

    B. Have students interview their parents about their jobs and share the findings in class.

    C. Ask parents to volunteer in the classroom on a rotating basis.

    D. Send home weekly newsletters with updates on classroom activities and upcoming events.

73. Ms. Patel wants to create a classroom environment that celebrates cultural diversity and promotes understanding among her students. Which of the following strategies would best achieve this goal?

    A. Include traditional music from various cultures in the classroom's daily playlist.

    B. Set up a cultural dress-up area where students can try on traditional clothing from different countries.

    C. Invite families for a Culture Day to share their cultural customs, stories, and traditions with the class.

    D. Decorate the classroom with flags from different countries around the world.

74. Ms. Turner is preparing her preschool students for the transition to kindergarten. Which strategy would best help the children transition to their new educational setting?

A. Send home reading materials that will be used in kindergarten.

B. Collaborate with the kindergarten teachers to send a welcome video to the preschool class.

C. Hold a parent meeting to discuss the academic expectations of kindergarten.

D. Organize a visit to the kindergarten classrooms, where students can meet the teachers and see the environment.

75. Ms. Thompson is implementing a Multi-Tiered System of Supports (MTSS) in her early childhood classroom. She uses data from universal screenings and ongoing assessments to identify students who may need additional help. Which of the following best describes the components and process of MTSS?

A. Provide intensive, individualized interventions for all students to ensure everyone gets the help they need.

B. Implement targeted interventions after students repeatedly fail to respond to the core curriculum.

C. Use high-quality, evidence-based instruction, then provide targeted and intensive interventions as needed.

D. Collaborate with families when students are identified as needing Tier 3 support.

76. Ms. Carter is a new early childhood educator who wants to ensure she adheres to high ethical standards and provides the best learning experiences for her students. Which approach would best support her professional development and adherence to ethical standards?

A. Reference her initial teacher training and experience to guide her professional conduct.

B. Consult with colleagues occasionally to discuss ethical dilemmas as they arise.

C. Review school policies and procedures annually to stay informed about ethical guidelines.

D. Join professional organizations to stay updated on new research and best practices.

77. During a kindergarten PLC meeting, teachers review data from universal screenings and identify several students who need additional support in reading. Which of the following actions best aligns with a Multi-Tiered System of Supports (MTSS) approach?

A. Provide extra reading homework to all students.

B. Increase the frequency of reading assessments for students who are struggling.

C. Implement small-group targeted interventions for the students needing support.

D. Wait until the end of the semester to reassess the students and intervene accordingly.

78. Mr. Smith, a first-grade teacher, is preparing for parent-teacher conferences and wants to discuss students' reading progress. Which strategy would be most effective for Mr. Smith during the conferences?

A. Present summative assessment data to show parents a broad view of their child's reading level.

B. Focus on formative assessment data and provide specific examples of student work to illustrate progress.

C. Discuss formative and summative assessment data, highlighting strengths and areas for improvement, and provide recommendations for at-home support.

D. Use the meeting to discuss classroom behavior and social skills instead of academic progress.

79. Ms. Davis, an early childhood educator, wants to better understand her students' backgrounds and needs to provide more individualized support. She decides to implement a strategy that aligns with the principles of the Individuals with Disabilities Education Act (IDEA). Which of the following approaches would best help Ms. Davis achieve this goal?

   A. Engage with parents and caregivers through home visits or community meetings to gain insights into children's backgrounds and needs

   B. Conduct classroom observations to identify students' academic strengths and weaknesses.

   C. Send home weekly newsletters to keep parents informed about classroom activities.

   D. Administer standardized tests to all students to gather data on their academic performance.

80. Mr. Johnson is a fourth-grade teacher who has a student, Emily, with a diagnosed hearing impairment. Which action should Mr. Johnson take to support Emily's needs?

   A. Assign Emily to the classroom's front row and provide her with a buddy to help with assignments.

   B. Ensure Emily's 504 Plan includes specific accommodations, such as providing an FM system and ensuring all instructional videos have captions.

   C. Arrange that Emily receive additional tutoring sessions after school to cover missed content.

   D. Implement a behavior intervention plan to address any classroom disruptions caused by Emily's hearing impairment.

81. Which of the following would **NOT** follow HIPAA?

   A. Posting student health information on the private staff electronic bulletin board for easy access for teachers only.

   B. Storing student health records in a locked cabinet and sharing information only with authorized personnel.

   C. Ensuring that student health information is discussed only with authorized staff members.

   D. Using secure electronic systems to share student health information with authorized healthcare providers.

82. Ms. Jordan and her colleagues form a data team to improve their instructional practices and student outcomes. Which of the following steps should the team take first to ensure a data-driven approach to identifying trends and developing action plans?

   A. Implement new instructional strategies based on their past experiences.

   B. Collect and analyze current student performance data to identify areas of need.

   C. Discuss opinions and insights on what might improve student performance.

   D. Schedule weekly meetings to share teaching resources.

83. Phonemic awareness includes the ability to:

   A. Form compound words and combine word parts.

   B. Spell accurately and decode unfamiliar words.

   C. Pronounce individual sounds in words.

   D. Differentiate between homonyms and spell accurately.

84. Students see the following image and say, "Bug!" What stage of word recognition are the students in?

- A. Pre-alphabetic
- B. Partial alphabetic
- C. Full-alphabetic
- D. Consolidated alphabetic

Use the following scenario to answer questions 85 and 86.

The teacher is working with students on words. She tells the students to say the word "hat." They all say the word "hat." Then she tells them to say the word "hat" with a /p/ sound in the beginning instead of the /h/ sound.

85. Which skill is the teacher working on with students?
- A. Phonics
- B. Fluency
- C. Comprehension
- D. Phonemic awareness

86. What strategy is the teacher using?
- A. Substitution
- B. Deletion
- C. Segmenting
- D. Isolation

87. A student sees the picture below. And writes the letters *S* and *N*.

SN

What would be the most appropriate next step in the spelling continuum?
- A. Print using lowercase letters
- B. Being to use medial vowel sounds
- C. Blend consonant sounds
- D. Recognize common sight words

88. Which is **NOT** a best practice for vocabulary instruction?

    A. Model using context clues

    B. Teaching prefixes, suffixes, and roots

    C. Explicit instruction using a dictionary

    D. Using word walls for target vocabulary

89. A teacher is helping students use the semantic cueing system. Which of the following questions aligns with the semantic cueing system?

    A. Is that structured properly?

    B. What sound does that letter make?

    C. Does that make sense?

    D. Is that a long /a/ sound or a short /a/ sound?

90. Ms. Gomez is working to support her kindergarten students' development of writing skills, particularly handwriting. Which strategies best demonstrate her knowledge of using manipulatives to enhance fine motor skills? Choose **ALL** that apply.

    ☐ A. Encouraging students to write full sentences on lined paper.

    ☐ B. Providing students with clay and playdough to strengthen their hand muscles.

    ☐ C. Asking students to copy words from the board onto paper.

    ☐ D. Using special grips on pencils to help students hold them correctly.

    ☐ E. Having students read aloud to improve their reading fluency.

91. Ms. Johnson is teaching her first-grade class to develop comprehension skills. Which of the following activities would best help students make text-to-self connections?

    A. Ask students to summarize the main events of a story.

    B. Have students draw a picture of their favorite character from the book.

    C. Encourage students to relate a personal experience like an event in the story.

    D. Ask students to identify the main idea of the text.

92. Which of the following strategies would best support students in making text-to-world connections during a reading lesson?

    A. Ask students to compare the characters in the story to themselves.

    B. Discuss how the story's events relate to current or historical events.

    C. Have students retell the story in their own words.

    D. Encourage students to create a timeline of the events in the story.

93. Match the stage of writing to the activity.

1.	writing strings of words
2.	writing his or her name
3.	scribbling in a pattern
4.	scribbling randomly

A.	preliterate
B.	emergent
C.	transitional
D.	fluent

94. A kindergarten teacher uses a large book in the front of the room and asks students, "Where should I begin reading this text?" The students point to the top left corner of the page. What skill is the teacher reinforcing?

   A. Phonological awareness

   B. Metacognition

   C. Concepts of print

   D. Prosody

95. Ms. Taylor wants to enhance her kindergarten classroom by creating a print-rich environment. Which of the following methods would best support this objective?

   A. Provide students with a robust classroom library where students can self-select books.

   B. Read aloud to the class daily while students listen quietly.

   C. Encourage students to bring books from home to read in class.

   D. Display students' stories on the bulletin board without their identifying information.

96. Ms. Johnson is a first-grade teacher who wants to improve her students' reading comprehension by helping them become more aware of their thinking processes while they read. Which of the following strategies would best support this goal?

   A. Assign daily independent reading time.

   B. Use "Read Aloud, Think Aloud" activities to model thought processes during reading.

   C. Encourage students to write summaries after reading a passage and have them share their summaries with the class.

   D. Have students take turns reading aloud to the class without interruption.

97. Ms. Lopez is preparing a lesson for her second-grade class on different types of animals. She wants to help her students organize their thoughts and clearly visualize the similarities and differences between mammals and reptiles. Which of the following graphic organizers would be most appropriate for this task?

   A. Venn Diagram

   B. Timeline

   C. Concept Map

   D. Flowchart

98. After reading "Arthur's Tooth" by Marc Brown to her first-grade class, Ms. Diaz wants to help her students make text-to-self connections. Which of the following questions would best encourage children to relate the text to their own experiences?

   A. "Have you ever lost a tooth? How did you feel about it?"

   B. "Can you describe Arthur's feelings about losing his tooth?"

   C. "What other books have you read about losing teeth?"

   D. "What do you think will happen to Arthur next?"

99. After introducing her first-grade class to the concept of integrating literacy across different content areas, Ms. Johnson wants to engage her students in an activity that combines reading and writing with other subjects. Which of the following activities would best support this integration?

   A. Ask students to share how they feel about the reading they did in social studies class.

   B. Have students complete a worksheet with science vocabulary and use the new words in a sentence.

   C. Encourage students to keep math journals where they write about their problem-solving processes.

   D. Have students work in groups to finish their art projects and then critique each other's work.

100. Mrs. Garcia reads "The True Story of the Three Little Pigs" by Jon Scieszka to her kindergarten class. She wants her students to understand how point of view can change a story. Which of the following activities would best help her students grasp this concept?

   A. Ask students to draw their favorite scene from the story.

   B. Have students act out the story as it was originally written.

   C. Encourage students to write a summary of the story.

   D. Discuss how the story changes when told from the wolf's perspective.

101. A teacher is using dice to help students recognize numbers. She rolls one di, and the students immediately say, "Three!" What skill are the students and teacher working on?

   A. Transitivity

   B. Patterns

   C. Subitizing

   D. Decomposition

102. Which of the following would be most appropriate for helping students to recognize patterns?

A.

C.

B.

D.

103. A teacher is helping students work towards the objective of classifying and categorizing geometric shapes. Which prerequisite skill must students master before they can meet this new objective?

A. Defining area

B. Drawing shapes

C. Recognizing shape attributes

D. Identifying patterns

104. A teacher is working with students on units of measurement. What would be the most effective activity to meet the objective below?

Students will use nonstandard units of measure to calculate length.

A. Have students measure their desks using paperclips.

B. Have students form a line from tallest student to shortest student.

C. Have students use a tape measure to measure the length and width of the room.

D. Have students work in cooperative groups to read about standard units of measure.

105. A teacher has students pick their favorite animal from a group of four: dog, dolphin, frog, and elephant. Then, based on everyone's preference, students create the chart below. What skill does this activity reinforce?

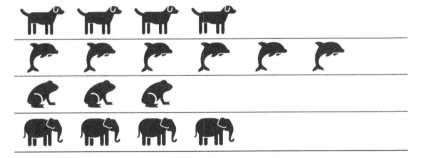

A. Pattern recognition

B. Decomposition of numbers

C. Data organization

D. Probability

106. What skill would the manipulative below be most effective in reinforcing?

- A. Fractions
- B. Order
- C. Patterns
- D. Base ten

107. A teacher is using the following word problem with students. Which skill does this word problem reinforce?

Jan has seven pieces of gum in her backpack. Sidney has four pieces in his backpack. How many more pieces of gum does Jan have than Sidney?

- A. Addition
- B. Subtraction
- C. Multiplication
- D. Division

108. A teacher uses the number below and asks, "What is the value of the underline number?"

345

What skill is the teacher working on?

- A. Multidigit numbers
- B. Estimation
- C. Subitizing
- D. Place value

109. A teacher has students use the diagram below to represent 25%. What skill is the teacher focusing on in this lesson?

- A. Understanding fractions represent division problems
- B. Understanding whole numbers can be decomposed to parts of numbers
- C. Understanding equivalent fractions equal the same amount
- D. Understanding fractions can be represented in a variety of ways

110. A teacher is showing students how to represent data in a variety of ways. She wants them to pick the most appropriate graph or chart to present a data set. Which of the following would be most appropriate for representing the percentage of students who like various flavors of ice cream—25% strawberry, 25% vanilla, and 50% chocolate?

    A. Line graph

    B. Bar graph

    C. Pictograph

    D. Circle graph

111. While completing an addition problem, the teacher has students use snap cubes to find the sum. Which instructional approach is the teacher using?

    A. Abstract

    B. Fluency

    C. Concrete

    D. Representational

112. A kindergarten teacher is beginning a lesson on the attributes of two-dimensional figures. Which of the following would be an appropriate strategy for the teacher to begin the lesson?

    A. Use dot paper or a geoboard to explore the attributes of figures.

    B. Make a table and list the attributes of two-dimensional figures.

    C. Use geometric formulas to determine the attributes of two-dimensional figures.

    D. Use base ten blocks to explore the attributes of two-dimensional figures.

113. Which of the following best depicts why 3 x 5 = 15?

114. Mr. Smith wants his kindergarten students to practice grouping and sorting objects based on attributes. He gives each student a handful of blue and green tiles and asks them to fill out the following sentences:

- I have _____ blue tiles.

- I have _____ green tiles.

- I have more _____ tiles than _____ tiles.

- I have _____ tiles in all.

Which of the following best explains the primary mathematical concept being taught in this activity?

A. Counting and Cardinality

B. Addition and Subtraction

C. Measurement and Data

D. Geometry

115. Mrs. Adams places several blocks in a row and asks students to identify the number of blocks. The students say five. Next, Ms. Adams rearranges them into a circle. She asks her students how many blocks are in the circle. All the students correctly identify that there are still five blocks.

Which of the following best explains the mathematical concept taught in this activity?

A. Pattern recognition

B. Spatial reasoning

C. Conservation of numbers

D. Addition and subtraction

116. Mr. Thompson works on developing math fact fluency with his third-grade students. He notices that some students can arrive at the correct answer quickly but cannot explain their method. Which aspect of math fact fluency should Mr. Thompson focus on to improve these students' skills?

A. Accuracy

B. Automaticity

C. Rate

D. Flexibility

117. Ms. Wilson's second-grade class has been practicing addition and subtraction facts. She wants to assess their fluency by focusing on their speed. Which aspect of math fact fluency is she primarily assessing?

A. Abstract

B. Automaticity

C. Rate

D. Flexibility

118. A teacher wants to assess her students' understanding of abstraction during a math lesson on counting. Which activity would best demonstrate this concept?

A. Ask students to count a set of identical red blocks.

B. Ask students to count a mixed set of blocks that vary in color, shape, and size.

C. Ask students to count by twos using a number line.

D. Ask students to recite the numbers from 1 to 20.

119. Ms. Green is teaching her first-grade class a new strategy to simplify addition. She explains that when adding 9 and 6, students can round 9 up to 10, add 10 and 6 to get 16 and subtract 1 to get the final answer of 15. What strategy is Ms. Green teaching her students?

   A. Subitizing

   B. One-to-one correspondence

   C. Pattern identification

   D. Compensation

120. Ms. Sanchez starts with the first addend, five, and then instructs her students to find the total number of books by subtracting. Which strategy could Ms. Sanchez use to help her students visualize this process?

   A. Subitizing

   B. Compensation

   C. One-to-one correspondence

   D. Using a number line

This page intentionally left blank.

Number	Category	Answer	Explanation
1.	I.	A	**Correct Answer A:** Thicker brushes and larger paper are easier for 3-year-olds to handle, supporting their developing fine motor skills. Older children can handle more precise tools and tasks. **Incorrect Answer B:** Giving both groups the same materials ignores the developmental differences between the two age groups. **Incorrect Answer C:** This option does not consider developmentally appropriate activities for each group of students. **Incorrect Answer D:** Avoiding actives is limiting and usually not the correct answer on the exam. Instead, teachers should modify activities so they are developmentally appropriate and so that all students get a chance to participate.
2.	I.	A	**Correct Answer A:** This modification allows the younger student to participate in a safe, developmentally appropriate environment. **Incorrect Answer B:** Giving both groups the same equipment ignores the developmental differences between the two age groups. **Incorrect Answer C:** Avoiding actives is limiting and usually not the correct answer on the exam. Instead, teachers should modify activities that are developmentally appropriate for all students to participate. **Incorrect Answer D:** This option is impractical in an early childhood classroom.
3.	I.	D	**Correct Answer D:** This activity is appropriate for assessing the fine motor development of a 4-year-old. It requires the use of hand muscles for cutting and controlling the scissors, which are key indicators of fine motor skills at this age. Children at age 4 begin to use scissors to cut simple things. **Incorrect Answer A:** This activity requires advanced fine motor control and letter formation skills that may be too difficult for a 4-year-old. **Incorrect Answer B:** This activity primarily involves gross motor skills. **Incorrect Answer C:** This activity is too advanced for a typical 4-year-old, as it requires a high level of precision and control in fine motor skills.

Practice Test 1

Number	Category	Answer	Explanation
4.	I.	D	**Correct Answer D:** Dancing to music is within the typical range of gross motor development for a 4-year-old. It involves coordination, balance, and movement, which are appropriate gross motor skills for this age group.
			Incorrect Answer A: This activity is typically more advanced and expected for children around 5 to 6 years old, as it requires precise fine motor coordination and dexterity.
			Incorrect Answer B: Writing complete sentences is a skill that generally develops later, often around 6 to 7 years old, as it involves both advanced fine motor skills and cognitive abilities.
			Incorrect Answer C: Playing a musical instrument involves complex fine motor skills and is usually beyond the capabilities of a 4-year-old.
5.	I.	A	**Correct Answer A:** Younger children often rely on trial and error to develop cognitive skills, whereas older children can apply more organized strategies based on experience and cognitive growth.
			Incorrect Answer B: Students of different age groups use different problem-solving skills. The eight-year-old will have more skills to use than the six-year-old will.
			Incorrect Answer C: Six-year-olds do not avoid puzzles. They will use different strategies to solve them than the eight-year-old.
			Incorrect Answer D: This may or may not be accurate. This option is too vague. Choice A outlines the reasons more effectively.
6.	I.	C	**Correct Answer C**: Older children are generally better at planning and strategizing due to more advanced cognitive development, whereas younger children often rely on experimentation.
			Incorrect Answer A: The term "refuse help" disqualifies this answer choice. While some children will try to figure it out independently, this is not true for all eight-year-olds.
			Incorrect Answer B: This choice uses strong language with the term "entirely." This is not true for all children. Avoid answer choices with strong language—never, only, entirely, etc.
			Incorrect Answer D: This choice switches the developmental capabilities of the two groups of children. Older children understand abstract concepts, while younger ones need concrete representation.
7.	I.	C	Cognitive ability results from the interaction of genetic and environmental influences, with neither acting in isolation. In addition, research has not concluded which one plays a more prominent role. When answering questions about this, remember that genetic and environmental aspects both play pivotal roles in cognitive ability.

Number	Category	Answer	Explanation
8.	I.	B & E	**Correct Answer B**: Providing various learning activities at different developmental stages demonstrates Ms. Hernandez's application of developmental knowledge. This strategy ensures that activities are tailored to meet the diverse needs of her students, supporting their growth and engagement. **Correct Answer E**: Practicing routines and procedures to maximize learning creates a structured environment that helps students feel secure and focused. This approach supports a healthy, respectful, and supportive classroom atmosphere. **Incorrect Answer A**: Implementing a strict discipline system to maintain order does not align with developmental knowledge. Strict discipline may create a fearful environment rather than a supportive one, hindering student engagement and growth. **Incorrect Answer C**: Allowing students to complete all tasks independently without teacher intervention can lead to frustration and disengagement for students who need guidance and support. Developmentally appropriate practices include scaffolding and teacher support. **Incorrect Answer D**: Focusing solely on academic achievement to maintain equity neglects the importance of social, emotional, and developmental needs. A balanced approach that addresses all aspects of student development is essential for creating a supportive and healthy learning environment.
9.	I.	D	**Correct Answer D:** Providing access to a school breakfast program can help address these issues. **Incorrect Answer A:** Claiming that Liam's nutrition and health likely have no impact on his development is incorrect. Nutrition and health are critical factors that influence a child's physical growth, cognitive abilities, and emotional stability. Ignoring these aspects can hinder his overall development and academic performance. **Incorrect Answer B:** Stating that poor nutrition and health only affect physical development and leave cognitive and emotional development unaffected is incorrect. Poor nutrition can lead to difficulties in concentration, memory, and emotional regulation, impacting Liam's learning and social interactions. **Incorrect Answer C**: While notifying the parents is important, placing the sole responsibility on them without providing immediate support in school (such as access to the breakfast program) may not effectively address Liam's needs. The parents may not have the resources to provide to Liam. Additionally, it is crucial to provide immediate support to ensure Liam can learn effectively while at school.

Number	Category	Answer	Explanation
10.	I.	C	Mr. Kim can gather useful information through parent-teacher conferences, community involvement, and non-confidential school records, maintaining respect for family privacy while gaining necessary insights to support his students. The other answer choices violate FERPA and general student privacy.
11.	I.	D	Using bilingual resources and maintaining open communication with Arjun's family can help Ms. Patel support his learning and ensure that his cultural and linguistic background is respected and integrated into his education. The other practices in the incorrect answer choices are not culturally responsive and should be avoided.
12.	I.	D	**Correct Answer D:** According to Maslow's hierarchy of needs, physiological needs such as food, water, and sleep are the most basic and must be met first before a person can focus on higher-level needs. **Incorrect Answer A:** Esteem needs, which include feelings of accomplishment and recognition, are higher-level needs that cannot be effectively addressed until basic physiological needs are met. **Incorrect Answer B:** Self-actualization needs, which involve achieving one's full potential and creativity, are the highest-level needs and are only pursued once all other needs are satisfied. **Incorrect Answer C:** Safety needs, which include personal security and stability, come after physiological needs in Maslow's hierarchy.
13.	I.	B	**Correct Answer B:** Creating a stable and predictable classroom environment with clear rules and routines addresses students' safety needs, which include the need for security and order. **Incorrect Answer A:** While encouraging group projects can help build a sense of belonging (social needs), it does not directly address safety needs. **Incorrect Answer C:** Praising academic achievements targets esteem needs, which are higher in Maslow's hierarchy and should be addressed after safety needs. **Incorrect Answer D:** Opportunities for creative expression relate to self-actualization needs, which are the highest level of needs and are addressed after physiological, safety, social, and esteem needs are met.

Practice Test 1

Number	Category	Answer	Explanation
14.	I.	B	**Correct Answer B**: Collaborating with the speech therapist ensures that Tommy's specific needs are met by integrating speech activities into his daily routine, aligning with his IEP goals. **Incorrect Answer A**: Creating a separate curriculum isolates Tommy from his peers and does not promote inclusive education. **Incorrect Answer C**: Skipping speech activities contradicts the purpose of the IEP, which is to address and support his speech delay. **Incorrect Answer D**: Expecting Tommy to follow the same activities without modifications ignores the individualized support outlined in his IEP.
15.	I.	A	**Correct Answer A**: Reviewing Emily's current performance data and preparing to discuss her progress and areas of need ensures that Mr. Lopez provides relevant and comprehensive input during the IEP meeting. **Incorrect Answer B**: Creating new goals without consulting other team members undermines the collaborative nature of the IEP process. **Incorrect Answer C**: Focusing solely on behavior and disregarding academic performance provides an incomplete picture of Emily's needs. **Incorrect Answer D**: Only discussing positive aspects may prevent the team from addressing important areas of improvement, which is essential for effective IEP planning.
16.	I.	C	**Correct Answer C:** Children at the preoperational stage (ages 2-7) can typically count to 10, recognize basic shapes, and understand one-to-one correspondence. During this stage, as described by Jean Piaget, children begin to use symbols to represent objects but do not yet understand concrete logic. They develop early number sense, including the ability to count and match objects with numbers (one-to-one correspondence), and can identify basic shapes. **Incorrect Answer A:** This does not include the other skills in the preoperational stage. **Incorrect Answer B:** This does not include the other skills in the preoperational stage. **Incorrect Answer D:** Performing multiplication is too advance for those in the preoperational stage.

Number	Category	Answer	Explanation
17.	I.	D	**Correct Answer D**: An Individualized Education Program (IEP) specifies the exact educational services and supports each student with disabilities is entitled to receive. By keeping the students in class during their scheduled occupational therapy sessions, Ms. Carter is not providing the necessary services as mandated by their IEPs. This non-compliance prevents the students from receiving the support critical to their development and learning. You may be tempted to choose option A. While the least restrictive environment (LRE) is important, the primary issue here is the failure to provide the required occupational therapy services as specified in the IEPs.
18.	I.	B	**Correct Answer B:** Maturational theory, primarily associated with Arnold Gesell, posits that development is a natural, biological process that occurs in predictable stages. This theory supports the idea of delaying kindergarten entry to ensure children are developmentally ready to learn, based on the belief that readiness comes with age and maturation. **Incorrect Answer A:** Psychoanalytic theory, primarily associated with Freud, focuses on the influence of unconscious desires and early childhood experiences on development. It does not specifically address the timing of school readiness based on natural development. **Incorrect Answer C:** Sociocultural theory, proposed by Vygotsky, emphasizes the importance of social interactions and cultural context in cognitive development. While it highlights the role of the environment and interactions, it does not focus on the natural maturation timeline. **Incorrect Answer D:** Behavioral theory, associated with Skinner and Pavlov, focuses on observable behaviors and the effects of reinforcement and punishment. It does not address the biological readiness for school but rather how behaviors can be shaped by the environment.
19.	I.	D	**Correct Answer D**: Olivia's consistent failure to turn in homework and inability to follow a sequence despite reminders indicates potential issues with organization or underlying learning difficulties that require further attention and intervention. **Incorrect Answer A**: While Alex struggles with math and frequently asks for help, this shows he is seeking assistance, and his challenges could be addressed with additional support and practice. **Incorrect Answer B**: Mia's disruptions, though problematic, are more related to classroom management and social behavior rather than a fundamental academic or developmental concern. **Incorrect Answer C**: Ethan's exaggeration of achievements reflects a desire for recognition and creativity, which are typical behaviors for his age and not a primary concern for academic or behavioral development.

Practice Test 1

Number	Category	Answer	Explanation
20.	I.	C	**Correct Answer C:** Encouraging students to test more objects and make predictions to understand why some objects float and others sink aligns with the constructivist approach and allows students to construct their own understanding through experimentation and inquiry, fostering deeper comprehension of buoyancy principles. **Incorrect Answer A:** While informative, explaining to the students that an object's buoyancy is related to its density compared to the density of water is more of a direct instructional method and does not engage students in the active learning process emphasized by constructivist principles. **Incorrect Answer B:** Showing a video that explains how the shape of an object can affect its ability to float is a passive learning activity. While it provides valuable information, it does not involve hands-on experimentation or active student participation. **Incorrect Answer D:** While asking students to draw pictures of floating objects and write about them in their journals is a reflective activity, it does not directly engage them in further experimentation or inquiry to deepen their understanding of buoyancy.
21.	I.	B	**Correct Answer B:** Teaching children to celebrate and appreciate each other's cultural backgrounds promotes inclusivity, respect, and emotional safety by helping children feel valued and understood. **Incorrect Answer A:** Organizing the classroom furniture to create clear pathways and reduce physical hazards is important for safety and accessibility, but it does not directly address creating an inclusive and supportive social environment. **Incorrect Answer C:** Providing a variety of art supplies for creative expression during free play encourages creativity and self-expression, but it does not specifically promote inclusivity and support for all cultural backgrounds. **Incorrect Answer D:** Creating a visual schedule to help children understand the daily routine aids in classroom management and supports children's understanding of structure, but it does not directly foster a socially supportive and inclusive environment.

Practice Test 1

Number	Category	Answer	Explanation
22.	I.	C	**Correct Answer C**: Engaging in extensive pretend play is characteristic of Piaget's preoperational stage (ages 2-7), where children develop symbolic thinking and use imagination to create scenarios and roles. **Incorrect Answer A**: Experimenting with objects by throwing them is more typical of the sensorimotor stage (ages 0-2), where children learn about the world through sensory exploration and physical interaction. **Incorrect Answer B**: Recognizing that others have different perspectives is a sign of moving towards the concrete operational stage (ages 7-11), where children begin to understand other viewpoints and develop theory of mind. **Incorrect Answer D**: Using logical thinking to solve puzzles is indicative of the concrete operational stage (ages 7-11), where children start to apply logical operations to concrete problems.
23.	I.	B	**Correct Answer B:** Setting up differentiated learning centers allows Ms. Thompson to provide a variety of activities that cater to different ability levels and learning styles, ensuring that all students are engaged and challenged appropriately. **Incorrect Answer A:** Giving all students the same worksheet with identical addition problems does not account for the diverse abilities and learning styles of the students. It may not provide adequate support or challenge for everyone. **Incorrect Answer C:** Delivering a lecture on addition principles and allowing time for questions is a one-size-fits-all approach that may not effectively address the varied learning needs of the students. **Incorrect Answer D:** Focusing on advanced students while letting others practice basic skills independently neglects the needs of students who may require additional support or different instructional strategies to grasp the concepts.

Number	Category	Answer	Explanation
24.	I.	A	**Correct Answer A:** By offering multiple means of representation, Mr. Rivera ensures that the reading material is accessible to all students, regardless of their developmental differences, aligning with UDL principles. This approach caters to various learning preferences and needs, making the lesson more inclusive. **Incorrect Answer B**: Providing a single reading passage for all students to read independently does not accommodate the diverse needs and abilities of the students. It limits access for those who may require different modes of representation. **Incorrect Answer C:** Delivering a lecture on the reading material and expecting all students to take notes and answer questions is a one-size-fits-all approach. It does not consider the varied learning styles and developmental differences within the class. **Incorrect Answer D:** Focusing on students with advanced reading skills and giving them additional challenging texts while others work on the standard passage neglects the needs of students who may require additional support or different instructional strategies. This approach does not promote inclusivity or accessibility for all students.
25.	I.	B	**Correct Answer B:** Integrating activities that promote movement, journal writing, role play, and speaking into the daily schedule best aligns with a holistic approach to teaching. This strategy addresses students' cognitive, social, emotional, physical, and language needs, ensuring a comprehensive developmental experience. **Incorrect Answer A:** Focusing on academic skills such as reading and math during classroom time does not encompass the holistic approach. This strategy neglects other critical areas of development, such as social, emotional, and physical growth. **Incorrect Answer C:** Using standardized tests and essay assignments to measure student progress and development is not aligned with a holistic approach. These methods primarily assess cognitive skills and do not consider the full spectrum of a child's development, including social, emotional, and physical aspects. **Incorrect Answer D:** Assigning independent study projects that students can design themselves and complete at their own pace does not support a holistic approach. This strategy limits opportunities for social interaction, emotional expression, and physical movement, and may not address the diverse needs of all students.
26.	II.	D	All the statements, except for answer D, are objective statements of behavior. Answer D, however, goes beyond describing Sarah's observable behaviors (sitting quietly and avoiding eye contact) and makes an inference about her emotional state (feeling lonely and isolated), which cannot be directly observed. This is called interference because it interferes with the objectivity of the statement of behavior.

Practice Test 1

Number	Category	Answer	Explanation
27.	II.	A	**Correct Answer A**: While the universal screening and the oral fluency identified the students as at risk, the teacher will need to use more assessments to pinpoint exactly where the students are having trouble. Using specific assessments to diagnose whether students are struggling with phonemic awareness, phonics, and morphology, and at what level will help the teacher differentiate instruction and prescribe interventions specific for each student's needs. **Incorrect Answer B**: This method jumps directly to a fluency exercise without knowing exactly what the students need. **Incorrect Answer C**: This describes homogenous grouping, which is typically a bad choice on the exam. **Incorrect Answer D**: The teacher must learn to diagnose and help students without relying on outside help.
28.	II.	D	The most important reason to use assessments is to make instructional decisions. Assessments can be used to assess the skills listed in the other answer choices. However, highly effective educators use assessments to make instructional decisions.
29.	II.	B	**Correct Answer B**: This is the most effective approach because a diagnostic pretest will give the teacher a baseline of where the students are. Formative assessments throughout the semester will help the teacher adjust instruction and strategies. Finally, a summative assessment at the end of the semester will measure the outcomes for the strategies used. This is the only answer choice that uses the proper assessments in the proper order and progression.
30.	II.	C	**Correct Answer C**: This option combines quantitative data (checklist of sight words) with qualitative data (anecdotal records), providing a comprehensive assessment of each child's literacy development. **Incorrect Answer A**: This relies solely on standardized test scores, providing quantitative data but lacks the contextual understanding provided by qualitative data. **Incorrect Answer B**: This uses only observational notes, giving qualitative insights but misses measurable evidence that quantitative data provides. **Incorrect Answer D**: This depends solely on qualitative data without quantitative support, which may result in an incomplete understanding of each child's literacy skills.

Number	Category	Answer	Explanation
31.	II.	A	**Correct answer A** – This method combines systematic observations, checklists and rubrics, and portfolios, ensuring that Ms. Turner gathers comprehensive and consistent data on her students' skills and competencies. None of the other options provide a comprehensive approach to assessment. Option B focuses just on diagnostic assessments. Option C focuses solely on quantitative assessment from state tests. Option D focuses only on anecdotal records.
32.	II.	D	Formative assessments are ongoing and used to monitor student learning and provide feedback for instructional adjustments. Methods include observations, exit tickets, think-pair-share, daily quizzes, and anecdotal records.
33.	II.	B	Criterion-Referenced assessments measure student performance against a fixed set of criteria or learning standards, such as the state's mathematics standards. This approach allows Ms. Johnson to determine if students meet the specific learning goals.
34.	II.	C	Performance-Based assessments require students to demonstrate their knowledge and skills through practical tasks like science experiments, presentations, role-playing, and art projects.
35.	II.	B	Anecdotal records are qualitative data that provide detailed, narrative descriptions of a student's behaviors and skills, capturing specific instances of what the student can do in different contexts.
36.	II.	D	Demonstrating one-to-one correspondence by matching objects to numbers directly assesses the children's understanding of numerical concepts, which is essential for learning formal mathematical symbols. Counting orally, classifying objects by shape, and grouping objects into sets do not specifically assess readiness for learning number symbols.
37.	II.	A	The teacher's role includes identifying potential speech difficulties, documenting observations, and communicating with parents and speech-language pathologists to ensure the child is referred for appropriate services. Diagnosing and prescribing therapies and conducting formal speech therapy sessions are the responsibility of the speech pathologist, not the teacher. Finally, waiting until parents notice an issue is not effective.

Number	Category	Answer	Explanation
38.	II.	A	A multidimensional assessment considers the diverse cultural and linguistic backgrounds of students, ensuring that their unique strengths and needs are identified and addressed comprehensively. All the other answer choices ignore the nature of a multidimensional assessment for students with cultural and linguistic differences.
39.	II.	B	**Correct Answer B**: This method combines quantitative data (rating scale) and qualitative data (journal of specific incidents), providing a well-rounded view of both social interactions and academic progress. **Incorrect Answer A**: While interviews provide qualitative data, they lack the quantitative measures needed for a comprehensive assessment. **Incorrect Answer C**: A math skills test offers quantitative data but does not provide insights into social interactions or qualitative aspects of student behavior. **Incorrect Answer D**: Tracking attendance provides quantitative data but does not assess social interactions or academic progress in a detailed manner.
40.	II.	B	**Correct Answer B**: The note in option B specifically provides information about Maria's counting skills and her understanding of number sense, which are crucial components of early childhood math. **Incorrect Answer A**: While sorting by color and shape is an important math skill, it does not directly assess counting or number sense. **Incorrect Answer C**: Measuring length is a valuable math skill, but it does not provide specific information about counting or number sense. **Incorrect Answer D**: Identifying shapes is a foundational math skill but does not address counting or number sense.

Number	Category	Answer	Explanation
41.	II.	D	**Correct Answer D**: Performance-based assessments enable students to showcase their math skills and knowledge through practical tasks. This method provides a more comprehensive view of what students understand and can do, as it involves applying their skills in real-world or simulated scenarios, rather than simply selecting answers from a list. **Incorrect Answer A**: Multiple-choice questions are not typically used in performance-based assessments. These questions can quickly assess knowledge but do not allow students to demonstrate practical application of skills. **Incorrect Answer B**: While standardized comparisons are valuable, they are characteristic of norm-referenced assessments, not performance-based assessments. **Incorrect Answer C**: Word problems are useful for assessing understanding, but performance-based assessments go beyond this by requiring students to engage in practical, hands-on tasks. Also, not all performance-based math problems focus only on word problems.
42.	II.	C	**Correct Answer C**: Standardized tests often fail to account for the diverse cultural and linguistic backgrounds of students, which can result in biased outcomes. These tests are typically designed with a specific population in mind, and when used with students from different cultural or linguistic backgrounds, they may not provide an accurate assessment of their abilities. **Incorrect Answer A**: Standardized tests are designed to provide consistent and reliable data that can be compared across different populations, although they may not be fair to all populations. **Incorrect Answer B**: While standardized tests may not delve deeply into individual critical thinking abilities, some standardized tests are written in a way that can assess critical thinking skills. This is also not the primary disadvantage of standardized assessments. **Incorrect Answer D**: Standardized tests are generally efficient and can be scored relatively quickly, allowing for timely use of the assessment data. The length of time required for evaluation is not a primary disadvantage.

Number	Category	Answer	Explanation
43.	II.	A, C, D & E	**Correct Answer A:** Providing written reports with detailed explanations helps parents understand the results and offers concrete suggestions for supporting their child at home. **Correct Answer Option C:** Holding face-to-face meetings or conferences allows for direct communication, addressing parents' questions and concerns immediately. **Correct Answer Option D:** Using visual aids, such as charts and graphs, makes complex information more accessible and easier to understand for parents. **Correct Answer Option E:** Offering workshops or informational sessions empowers parents with the knowledge to interpret assessment results and effectively support their child's learning. **Incorrect Answer B:** Only showing the data that parents can understand leaves out important information about their child's progress. All data should be shared, and it is the teacher's job to communicate it clearly and effectively so parents can comprehend the information.
44.	II.	B	**Correct Answer B:** Triangulation involves using multiple data sources to ensure a comprehensive and accurate understanding of student performance. By combining observations, student work samples, and standardized test scores, Mr. Martinez can confirm his findings and obtain a more complete picture of each student's abilities and progress. **Incorrect Answer A:** Relying solely on standardized test scores, even for evaluating multiple aspects of performance, does not utilize multiple data sources, which is essential for triangulation. **Incorrect Answer C:** While using anecdotal records over the school year provides valuable qualitative data, it does not incorporate the multiple data sources necessary for triangulation. **Incorrect Answer D:** Administering multiple-choice quizzes and averaging scores focuses on a single assessment method and does not provide the multi-faceted approach needed for triangulation.
45.	III.	B	**Correct Answer B:** This aligns with the LRE principles by including students with disabilities in the general classroom and providing the necessary supports and accommodations to ensure they can participate fully and effectively. **Incorrect Answer A:** Creating a separate classroom segregates students with disabilities does not align with the LRE principles of inclusion and integration. **Incorrect Answer C:** Placing students in the general classroom without supports does not address their individual needs and can hinder their ability to learn and participate effectively. **Incorrect Answer D:** Typically, teachers do not have the authority or access to assign dedicated aids to students.

Number	Category	Answer	Explanation
46.	III.	C	**Correct Answer C:** This method describes a picture walk to activate background knowledge. A picture walk involves looking at the pictures in a book before reading the text, which helps students make predictions and access their prior knowledge. This strategy effectively engages students and prepares them for the content they will encounter in the story. **Incorrect Answer A:** While integrating information about frogs into different subjects can reinforce learning it does not specifically access students' prior knowledge before reading the book. **Incorrect Answer B:** Demonstrating how to use a big book to teach concepts of print like directionality is a valuable literacy activity, but it does not directly assess students' prior knowledge about frogs. **Incorrect Answer D:** Presenting scientific facts is developmentally appropriate, but not as engaging for young children as a picture walk. Using pictures allows for more interactive and reflective thinking.
47.	III.	A	**Correct Answer A:** An Individualized Education Program (IEP) is a legal document that outlines specific educational accommodations, services, and supports that must be provided to students with disabilities. By not sending the students to their scheduled occupational therapy sessions, Ms. Rodriguez is in violation of the IEPs, which must be followed under federal law (IDEA – Individuals with Disabilities Education Act). **Incorrect Answer B:** While failing to follow an IEP could be seen as discriminatory, the primary issue is the legal requirement to provide the services specified in the IEP. **Incorrect Answer C:** Teachers do not have the authority to override the provisions of an IEP. Ensuring adequate reading instruction is important, but it cannot replace the required occupational therapy services. **Incorrect Answer D:** Even with permission from the occupational therapist, the IEP must be followed unless it is formally amended through the proper IEP team process, which includes parental consent and participation.

Number	Category	Answer	Explanation
48.	III.	C	**Correct Answer C**: Demonstrating how to plant seeds and care for them, and allowing the children to practice, provides a hands-on learning experience. This approach helps students understand the process through direct involvement, making the lesson more engaging and memorable. **Incorrect Answer A**: While discussing the benefits of a gardening career might be interesting, it does not provide a practical demonstration of planting and caring for plants, which is the focus of the unit. **Incorrect Answer B**: Distributing seeds and plant pots is helpful, but without a demonstration, children may not understand how to use the materials effectively. **Incorrect Answer D**: Showing pictures of neglected plants can illustrate the importance of plant care, but it does not provide the hands-on experience necessary for young learners to grasp the planting process.
49.	III.	B, D & E	**Correct Answer B**: Setting a rotating schedule for students to feed the fish, clean the tank, and record observations ensures that all students are involved and learn about responsibility. This strategy uses developmentally appropriate practices by providing structure, clear expectations, and hands-on learning experiences. **Correct Answer D**: Demonstrating how to care for the fish with detailed step-by-step explicit instructions helps students understand the specific tasks involved and provides a clear model for them to follow, enhancing their ability to care for the fish effectively. **Correct Answer E**: Establishing a routine for feeding and caring for the fish, and making it part of the daily classroom schedule, provides consistency and helps students develop a sense of responsibility and reliability. **Incorrect Answer A**: Placing the fish tank next to the computer and listening stations may cause distractions due to the noise from the headsets and electronic activities, which can interfere with the quiet observation needed for studying the fish. **Incorrect Answer C**: Allowing only a few selected students to care for the fish limits the learning opportunity for other students and does not promote inclusion and equal responsibility. **Incorrect Answer F**: Placing the fish tank in a corner of the room minimizes interaction and observational opportunities, which are crucial for learning about aquatic life and developing responsibility through hands-on experience.

Number	Category	Answer	Explanation
50.	III.	B	**Correct Answer B**: Using counting bears (manipulatives) to show how adding bears to a group and taking bears away from a group changes the total number provides a hands-on, visual way for young children to understand the concepts of addition and subtraction, making the abstract ideas concrete and understandable. Remember, using manipulatives in early childhood is always a best practice. **Incorrect Answer A**: Giving students worksheets with addition and subtraction problems does not provide the hands-on, manipulative-based learning that is most effective for prekindergarten students. **Incorrect Answer C**: While videos can be informative, they do not offer the hands-on experience that manipulatives provide, which is crucial for young learners to grasp mathematical concepts. **Incorrect Answer D**: Reading a story about numbers and asking students to draw pictures can be a supportive activity, but it does not directly engage students in the physical manipulation of objects to understand "put together" and "take away" concepts.
51.	III.	C	**Correct Answer C**: This question encourages children to think critically about their work and apply principles of observation and creativity to improve their sculptures, fostering deeper understanding and skill development. **Incorrect Answer A**: This question focuses on a basic counting skill rather than encouraging critical thinking and application of observation principles. **Incorrect Answer B**: While this question prompts children to reflect on their material choices, it does not engage them in applying observation or creativity principles. **Incorrect Answer D**: This question encourages comparison but does not specifically guide children to apply principles of observation and creativity to enhance their work.
52.	III.	B	**Correct Answer B**: This question encourages the student to explain their thinking process, which is a developmentally appropriate practice. It allows the teacher to understand the student's reasoning and provides an opportunity for guided learning without directly correcting the student. **Incorrect Answer A**: While this statement addresses the mistake, it does not help the student understand why their choice was incorrect or encourage further thinking. **Incorrect Answer C**: This statement provides a hint but might be too abstract for the student to understand without further context or explanation. **Incorrect Answer D**: This approach does not allow the student to think through the problem independently and learn from their mistake, which is less effective for development at this stage.

Number	Category	Answer	Explanation
53.	III.	A	**Correct Answer A**: At two years old, Max's language skills are still developing, and his use of simplified phrases is normal for his age. Over time, with exposure to proper language use, his speech will naturally become more complex. Answer A is the most developmentally appropriate. **Incorrect Answer B**: Correcting Max immediately and asking him to repeat the sentence correctly can discourage Max and make him self-conscious about speaking, which is not supportive of his natural language development. **Incorrect Answer C**: Creating a series of lessons on sentence structure for the entire class is not developmentally appropriate for two-year-olds, who learn best through natural interactions and play rather than formal lessons. **Incorrect Answer D**: While involving parents is important, this scenario does not warrant formal intervention; Max's speech is typical for his age.
54.	III.	D	**Correct Answer D**: This selection includes materials with distinct physical characteristics that children can touch and explore to understand concepts like texture, softness, and smoothness. **Incorrect Answer A**: While this selection is multisensory, it does not provide a varied range of physical characteristics for tactile exploration. **Incorrect Answer B**: This selection is effective for learning about nature and environments but is less focused on physical characteristics of objects. **Incorrect Answer C**: Although these materials have different physical properties, they do not offer the same tactile variety as the correct answer, which is more effective for exploring concepts like texture and smoothness.
55.	III.	D	**Correct Answer D**: This placement ensures that the vision-impaired student can see the teacher clearly, benefits from proper lighting, and has access to materials that support their learning needs. **Incorrect Answer A**: This placement does not support the visual needs of the student and may isolate them from the main instructional area. **Incorrect Answer B**: While natural light can be beneficial, it is important to control glare, and standard-sized materials may not be accessible for a vision-impaired student. **Incorrect Answer C**: This placement may not provide the best visual access to the teacher and instructional materials, and the use of auditory aids alone is insufficient for a vision-impaired student.

Practice Test 1

Number	Category	Answer	Explanation
56.	III.	B	**Correct Answer B**: This sequence follows the "I do, we do, you do" model, where the teacher starts by modeling the task, then supports students through guided practice, and finally allows them to practice independently. **Incorrect Answer A**: This sequence is not consistent with the gradual release of responsibility model. **Incorrect Answer C**: This sequence does not follow the "I do, we do, you do" model and lacks the initial direct instruction needed to scaffold learning. **Incorrect Answer D**: This approach does not provide the necessary scaffolding through direct instruction and guided practice.
57.	III.	A	**Correct Answer A**: This strategy effectively differentiates instruction by addressing the varied needs and abilities of students, ensuring all students receive appropriate levels of support. **Incorrect Answer B**: This approach does not differentiate instruction during regular class time and may not adequately support all students. **Incorrect Answer C**: While it adjusts the reading level, it does not provide the differentiated instructional support necessary for each group's needs. **Incorrect Answer D**: This strategy does not offer tailored support based on individual student needs and relies too heavily on whole-group instruction.
58.	III.	A	**Correct Answer A**: Why do you think the caterpillar turns into a butterfly? This open-ended question prompts students to think deeply and explore biological processes, stimulating critical thinking. **Incorrect Answer B**: This is a factual question that does not require critical thinking or exploration. **Incorrect Answer C**: This question is factual and recall-based, not encouraging deeper thinking or inquiry. **Incorrect Answer D**: This is a straightforward factual question that does not engage students in critical thinking or exploration.

Practice Test 1

Number	Category	Answer	Explanation
59.	III.	D	**Correct Answer D**: This activity exemplifies PBL by engaging students in a real-world problem that requires them to apply their mathematical skills. It encourages students to analyze, calculate, and make decisions based on their understanding of addition and subtraction. **Incorrect Answer A**: While this activity involves problem-solving, it does not provide a real-world context or require the depth of analysis that characterizes PBL. Also, the term "worksheet" is typically a bad word and not the correct answer on teacher certification exams. **Incorrect Answer B**: This activity focuses on rote memorization rather than critical thinking and problem-solving. **Incorrect Answer C**: Quizzes typically assess students' recall of information but does not engage them in the type of inquiry and problem-solving typical of PBL.
60.	III.	C	**Correct Answer C**: This activity engages students in hands-on learning and experimentation, encouraging them to make observations, analyze results, and develop critical-thinking skills. **Incorrect Answer A**: While discussing vocabulary can be beneficial, it does not involve hands-on exploration or experimentation, which are key for developing critical-thinking skills. **Incorrect Answer B**: Although watching a documentary and answering questions can be educational, it is a passive activity that does not engage students in active exploration or experimentation. **Incorrect Answer D**: This activity involves reading and note-taking, which are important skills, but not the hands-on, exploratory experience needed to develop critical-thinking skills.
61.	III.	C	**Correct Answer C**: This strategy exemplifies blended learning by integrating traditional classroom instruction with online components, providing students with the flexibility to work at their own pace and receive personalized support. **Incorrect Answer A**: This strategy does not blend traditional and online learning for the same subjects, thus not fully representing blended learning. **Incorrect Answer B**: While this incorporates online learning, it assumes that all students have access to technology at home, which may not be the case, potentially leading to inequality in learning opportunities. **Incorrect Answer D**: Although this uses technology, it does not integrate traditional classroom instruction with online learning in a blended manner.

Number	Category	Answer	Explanation
62.	III.	A	**Correct Answer A**: This strategy provides a structured and predictable environment that helps children understand and follow routines, developing self-regulation and independence. **Incorrect Answer B**: While promoting flexibility can be beneficial, it may not provide the consistent structure needed for young children to develop self-regulation and independence. **Incorrect Answer C**: While this approach can reinforce positive behavior, it does not necessarily help children develop self-regulation and independence through understanding and following routines. **Incorrect Answer D**: Although a predictable schedule is important, focusing heavily on consequences does not foster the development of self-regulation and independence in a supportive manner.
63.	III.	B	**Correct Answer B**: This strategy allows the classroom to be easily reconfigured to accommodate various planned activities, promoting a dynamic and adaptable learning environment. **Incorrect Answer A**: Fixed furniture does not provide the flexibility needed to accommodate different activities effectively. **Incorrect Answer C**: While this provides structure, it does not offer the flexibility to adapt the space for a variety of activities. **Incorrect Answer D**: A static layout limits the ability to adapt the environment to different activities and does not support a dynamic, flexible classroom.
64.	IV.	B	**Correct Answer B**: This approach supports the student within the general education setting, promoting inclusion and integration with peers. **Incorrect Answer A**: This option does not align with LRE principles as it removes the student from the general education environment unnecessarily. **Incorrect Answer C**: This segregates the student from their peers during crucial instructional periods, which is contrary to LRE guidelines. **Incorrect Answer D**: This reduces the student's opportunity for social interaction and inclusion, which are important aspects of LRE.

Number	Category	Answer	Explanation
65.	IV.	D	**Correct Answer D**: FERPA protects the privacy of student education records and sharing them with a parent volunteer would violate this law. **Incorrect Answer A**: This would violate FERPA regulations, as it involves sharing confidential student information without proper consent. **Incorrect Answer B**: While obtaining consent is important, FERPA typically limits the sharing of educational records to school officials with legitimate educational interests. **Incorrect Answer C**: Parent-teacher conferences should be conducted with the parents or guardians of the student, not with a parent volunteer.
66.	IV.	B	**Correct Answer B**: This activity aligns with the core purpose of PLCs, which is to enhance teaching practices and student outcomes through collaboration and data-driven discussions. **Incorrect Answer A**: While planning social events is beneficial, it does not reflect the primary focus of a PLC on instructional improvement and student progress. **Incorrect Answer C**: Learning about new tools is useful, but without application and follow-up, it does not fulfill the ongoing collaborative and data-driven nature of a PLC. **Incorrect Answer D**: While important, this activity is more administrative and does not directly address the instructional focus and student-centered goals of a PLC.
67.	IV.	A	**Correct Answer A**: Collaborating with colleagues and paraprofessionals allows for sharing insights and effective strategies that can address Emily's specific needs. **Incorrect Answer B**: While administrative support is important, this does not specifically address understanding Emily's reading comprehension needs. **Incorrect Answer C**: Transferring a student without first attempting to understand and address their needs is not a constructive approach. **Incorrect Answer D**: Delegating responsibilities is not the primary goal of conferring with colleagues and paraprofessionals; the focus should be on collaborative problem-solving and support.

Practice Test 1

Number	Category	Answer	Explanation
68.	IV.	A	**Correct Answer A**: This technique allows Ms. Rivera to critically analyze her practices and identify areas for improvement. **Incorrect Answer B**: While this can provide useful feedback, it is not a self-assessment technique that directly helps Ms. Rivera reflect on her own practices. **Incorrect Answer C**: This approach does not provide a comprehensive view of her teaching practices throughout the year. **Incorrect Answer D**: While observing peers can be beneficial, it is not a self-assessment technique focused on reflecting on her own practices.
69.	IV.	C	**Gross motor skills** – skills used in the torso, legs and arms. These include big movements like running, jumping, skipping, etc. **Fine motor skills** – skills used in the hands, fingers, feet, and toes. These include small movements like, using a pencil, buttoning a shirt, grasping utensils, etc. **Correct Answer C**: A physical therapist specializes in addressing gross motor delays such as difficulties with running, jumping, and balancing through targeted exercises and activities. **Incorrect Answer A**: Occupational therapists focus on fine motor skills, such as writing or buttoning a shirt, rather than gross motor skills. **Incorrect Answer B**: Speech therapists focus on communication and language skills, not on motor development. **Incorrect Answer D**: Paraprofessionals provide general support in the classroom but do not have the specialized training required to address gross motor delays.
70.	IV.	C	**Correct Answer C**: This combination provides multiple channels for timely, consistent, and interactive communication with parents, helping to keep them informed and engaged with their child's education. **Incorrect Answer A**: While newsletters can be helpful, they do not offer the immediacy and interactivity of real-time communication technologies. **Incorrect Answer B**: Although virtual conferences are useful, they are not as comprehensive for ongoing communication as a combination of a class website, emails, and a mobile app. **Incorrect Answer D**: YouTube, social media, and blogs might be beneficial for other purposes but are not the most appropriate tools for consistent, secure, and real-time communication with parents.

Number	Category	Answer	Explanation
71.	IV.	A, B, D, E & F	**Correct Answer A**: Surveys can provide valuable insights without breaching individual privacy when they are designed to collect general rather than personal information. **Correct Answer B**: Observations can offer important clues about a student's background and needs without directly asking invasive questions. **Correct Answer D**: These professionals can share important information within the bounds of confidentiality. **Correct Answer E**: These records provide context about the student's background that has been documented with privacy considerations. **Correct Answer F**: Conferences provide a private setting for parents to share information directly with the teacher. **Incorrect Answer C**: This approach could violate privacy and make students uncomfortable.
72.	IV.	A	**Correct Answer A**: This activity invites families into the classroom, allows them to see their children's work, and provides a relaxed setting for building relationships. **Incorrect Answer B**: While this engages families, it does not create a welcoming environment or build partnerships as effectively as involving families directly in school activities. **Incorrect Answer C**: This might create pressure on families who cannot easily volunteer due to work or other commitments. **Incorrect Answer D**: Newsletters are informative but do not actively engage families in a welcoming environment or promote partnerships in the same way as in-person events.
73.	IV.	C	**Correct Answer C**: This strategy engages families and provides students with direct, meaningful interactions that enhance their understanding and appreciation of diverse cultures. **Incorrect Answer A**: While this exposes students to different cultures, it lacks the interactive and personal element that fosters deeper understanding. **Incorrect Answer B**: Although this can be fun and educational, it does not provide the same level of engagement and firsthand learning as involving families directly. **Incorrect Answer D**: This visual approach is a good start but does not offer the interactive and experiential learning that helps students truly appreciate cultural diversity.

Practice Test 1

Number	Category	Answer	Explanation
74.	IV.	D	**Correct Answer D**: This hands-on approach allows children to become familiar with the new setting, reducing anxiety and helping them understand what to expect. **Incorrect Answer A**: While this can help with academic preparation, it does not address the child's need to become familiar with the new environment and routines. **Incorrect Answer B**: Although helpful, a video does not provide the same level of engagement and familiarity as an in-person visit. **Incorrect Answer C**: While important for parents, this strategy does not directly help children become familiar with the new environment, routines, and expectations.
75.	IV.	C	**Correct Answer C**: This answer accurately reflects the tiered approach of MTSS, starting with universal supports and progressing to more intensive interventions. **Incorrect Answer A**: This approach is not feasible or necessary for all students; MTSS starts with universal supports and targets interventions based on student needs. **Incorrect Answer B**: MTSS emphasizes early identification and support through universal screening and ongoing assessments, not waiting for failure. **Incorrect Answer D**: Family collaboration is important at all levels of MTSS, not just at the most intensive tier.
76.	IV.	D	**Correct Answer D**: Joining professional organizations like the National Association for the Education of Young Children (NAEYC) and the Division of Early Childhood (DEC) ensures that Ms. Carter stays informed about the latest developments in early childhood education and adheres to the highest ethical standards. **Incorrect Answer A**: Relying solely on her initial teacher training and experience is not enough. Ongoing professional development is crucial for staying current with best practices and ethical guidelines. **Incorrect Answer B**: Although valuable, this approach is not as comprehensive as engaging with professional organizations that provide continuous learning opportunities and updated resources. **Incorrect Answer C**: This is important but not sufficient on its own. Engaging with professional organizations provides a broader and more current perspective on ethical standards and best practices.

Number	Category	Answer	Explanation
77.	IV.	C	**Correct Answer C**: This aligns with tier 2 of MTSS, which focuses on providing targeted interventions for students who need additional help. **Incorrect Answer A**: This approach does not target the specific needs of the students identified. **Incorrect Answer B**: While ongoing assessments are important, targeted interventions are necessary for the identified students. **Incorrect Answer D**: Immediate interventions are crucial to support the students' progress.
78.	IV.	C	**Correct Answer C**: This approach gives a comprehensive view of the student's progress and specific ways parents can help at home. **Incorrect Answer A**: While important, focusing solely on summative data does not provide a complete picture of the student's progress. **Incorrect Answer B**: This is helpful but not comprehensive without the summative data for context. **Incorrect Answer D**: While important, this approach ignores the academic focus of the conference.
79.	IV.	A	**Correct Answer A**: This approach helps Ms. Davis understand the individual needs of her students, which is in line with the collaborative and inclusive principles of IDEA. **Incorrect Answer B**: While useful, this does not provide the same depth of understanding of students' backgrounds and needs as direct engagement with their families. **Incorrect Answer C**: This is a good communication strategy but does not gather insights into students' backgrounds and needs. **Incorrect Answer D**: This approach focuses on academic data rather than understanding the broader context of students' lives.

Number	Category	Answer	Explanation
80.	IV.	B	**Correct Answer B**: Ensuring Emily's 504 Plan includes specific accommodations, such as providing an FM system aligns with Section 504's requirement to outline specific accommodations that allow the child to access the curriculum and school environment effectively. **Incorrect Answer A**: Assigning Emily to the front row and providing her with a buddy is helpful but does not comprehensively address her specific needs as outlined in a 504 Plan. **Incorrect Answer C**: Additional tutoring sessions after school may help with academic support but do not constitute the necessary accommodations under a 504 Plan to access the regular curriculum. **Incorrect Answer D**: A behavior intervention plan is not appropriate for addressing the needs arising from Emily's hearing impairment and does not align with the purpose of a 504 Plan, which focuses on providing access and accommodations. **Quick Tip** Frequency Modulation (FM) systems are assistive listening devices designed to help individuals with hearing impairments by enhancing the clarity of sound in noisy environments. FM systems are commonly used in educational settings to support students with hearing difficulties.
81.	IV.	A	**Correct Answer A:** Posting student health information on the private staff electronic bulletin board for easy access for teachers only is not compliant with HIPAA regulations. Even though it is intended for teachers, it does not adequately protect the confidentiality of student health information. **Incorrect Answer B:** Storing student health records in a locked cabinet and sharing information only with authorized personnel is compliant with HIPAA regulations as it ensures the confidentiality and security of health information. **Incorrect Answer C:** Ensuring that student health information is discussed only with authorized staff members is compliant with HIPAA regulations as it restricts access to confidential information to authorized personnel. **Incorrect Answer D:** Using secure electronic systems to share student health information with authorized healthcare providers is compliant with HIPAA regulations as it ensures that information sharing is done securely and for legitimate purposes.

Number	Category	Answer	Explanation
82.	IV.	B	**Correct Answer B:** Collecting and analyzing current student performance data to identify areas of need is the most effective first step in a data-driven approach. It ensures that the team's action plans are based on actual evidence and trends from the data. **Incorrect Answer A:** Implementing new instructional strategies immediately based on past experiences does not use a data-driven approach and may not address the specific needs identified through data analysis. **Incorrect Answer C:** Discussing personal opinions on what might improve student performance is subjective and may not be based on the actual data trends, which can lead to less effective action plans. **Incorrect Answer D:** Scheduling weekly meetings to share teaching resources without focusing on data does not align with the goal of using data to drive instructional improvements and may lead to unfocused and ineffective strategies.
83.	V.	C	**Correct Answer C:** Phonemic awareness is understanding the individual sounds—or phonemes—in words. When you see the word *phonemic*, think of the root word *phone*, which is related to sound. **Incorrect Answer A:** While forming compound words and combining word parts are related to phonological awareness, they are not specific to phonemic awareness, which focuses on the ability to hear and manipulate individual sounds in words. **Incorrect Answer B:** Accurate spelling and decoding unfamiliar words are related to phonics, which involves understanding the relationship between sounds and their corresponding letters, but they are not specific to phonemic awareness. **Incorrect Answer D:** Differentiating between homonyms and spelling accurately pertain more to vocabulary and phonics skills rather than phonemic awareness, which is specifically about recognizing and manipulating individual sounds in words.

Number	Category	Answer	Explanation
84.	V.	A	**Correct Answer A:** At the pre-alphabetic stage, children recognize words as icons or visual symbols rather than through their alphabetic components. They often rely on visual cues, such as pictures or familiar logos, to identify words, as seen when students say "bug" upon seeing the image of a bug. **Incorrect Answer B:** At the partial alphabetic stage, students begin to recognize some letters and their sounds but still rely heavily on visual cues. While they might know some letters in a word, they would not yet be able to identify a word like "bug" purely based on the image. **Incorrect Answer C:** In the full-alphabetic stage, students can decode words using their knowledge of the complete letter-sound correspondences. They can recognize words by their alphabetic components rather than relying on visual cues. **Incorrect Answer D:** In the consolidated alphabetic stage, students recognize larger chunks of words, such as morphemes, and can read words more fluently. They no longer depend on visual symbols to identify words, indicating a more advanced stage of word recognition.
85.	V.	D	**Correct Answer D:** Phonemic awareness is the ability to hear, identify, and manipulate individual sounds (phonemes) in spoken words. The teacher's activity involves changing the initial sound in "hat" to /p/, which is a clear example of phonemic manipulation, a key component of phonemic awareness. **Incorrect Answer A:** Phonics involves the relationship between sounds and their spellings, which is not the focus of this activity. **Incorrect Answer B:** Fluency refers to the ability to read text smoothly and accurately, which is not being addressed in this activity. **Incorrect Option C:** Comprehension involves understanding the meaning of text, which is not the focus here.
86.	V.	A	**Correct Answer A:** Substitution involves replacing one sound in a word with another sound. The teacher is asking the students to substitute the /h/ sound in "hat" with a /p/ sound, turning "hat" into "pat." **Incorrect Answer A:** Deletion involves removing a sound from a word, which is not what the teacher is doing in this activity. **Incorrect Answer A:** Segmenting involves breaking a word into its individual sounds or phonemes, which is not the focus here. **Incorrect Answer A:** Isolation involves identifying individual sounds in a word, such as the first, middle, or last sound, which is not what the teacher is doing in this activity.

Number	Category	Answer	Explanation
87.	V.	B	**Correct Answer B:** The student's writing "SN" indicates that they can identify the initial and final consonant sounds but are missing the medial vowel sound. The next appropriate step in their spelling development is to help them begin to recognize and use medial vowel sounds, which will allow them to spell simple CVC (consonant-vowel-consonant) words correctly. **Incorrect Answer A:** While using lowercase letters is important, it is not the immediate next step in the spelling continuum for this student, who needs to focus on vowel sounds. **Incorrect Answer C:** The student is already demonstrating an ability to blend consonant sounds, as shown by writing "SN" for "sun." The gap is in recognizing and using the medial vowel. **Incorrect Answer D:** Recognizing common sight words is a different skill that involves memorizing whole words rather than focusing on the phonetic spelling patterns that this student needs to develop.
88.	V.	C	**Correct Answer C:** While dictionaries can be useful tools, relying solely on explicit instruction using a dictionary is not considered a best practice for effective vocabulary instruction. This method may not engage students actively or help them fully understand and retain new vocabulary words in meaningful contexts. **Incorrect Answer A:** Modeling how to use context clues helps students infer the meanings of unfamiliar words based on surrounding text, which is a valuable skill for vocabulary development. **Incorrect Answer B:** Teaching prefixes, suffixes, and roots helps students understand word structures and derive meanings of new words, aiding in vocabulary expansion. **Incorrect Answer D:** Using word walls for target vocabulary visually reinforces new words and concepts, providing students with a reference that supports ongoing learning and review.
89.	V.	C	**Correct Answer C:** The semantic cueing system involves using the meaning of words and sentences to help decode text. Asking "Does that make sense?" encourages students to think about whether the text fits logically and contextually within the passage, aligning with the semantic cueing system. **Incorrect Answer A:** This question aligns more with the syntactic cueing system, which focuses on the structure and grammar of the sentence. **Incorrect Answer B:** This question aligns with the phonological cueing system, which involves the sounds that letters and letter combinations make. **Incorrect Answer D:** This question also relates to the graphophonic cueing system, focusing on the pronunciation of vowel sounds based on letter-sound correspondence rather than the meaning of the text.

Practice Test 1

Number	Category	Answer	Explanation
90.	V.	B and D	**Correct Answer B:** Providing students with clay and playdough helps develop and strengthen hand muscles, which are essential for fine motor skills and handwriting. **Correct Answer D:** Using special grips on pencils helps students hold the pencils correctly, supporting proper handwriting technique and improving fine motor control. **Incorrect Answer A:** Encouraging students to write full sentences on lined paper practices handwriting but does not specifically involve manipulatives to develop fine motor skills. **Incorrect Answer C:** Asking students to copy words from the board focuses on handwriting practice but does not utilize manipulatives to support fine motor development. **Incorrect Answer E:** Reading aloud improves reading fluency but is not related to developing fine motor skills or handwriting.
91.	V.	C	**Correct Answer C:** Making text-to-self connections involves relating personal experiences to events or characters in the story, helping students understand and engage with the text on a personal level. **Incorrect Answer A:** Summarizing main events helps with comprehension but does not specifically focus on making personal connections. **Incorrect Answer B:** Drawing a favorite character can help with visualization but does not directly involve making connections to the student's own life. **Incorrect Answer D:** Identifying the main idea is a comprehension skill but does not involve relating the text to personal experiences.
92.	V.	B	**Correct Answer B:** Making text-to-world connections involves relating the content of the text to real-world events or historical contexts, helping students see the relevance of what they are reading to the larger world. **Incorrect Answer A:** Comparing characters to themselves helps with text-to-self connections, not text-to-world connections. **Incorrect Answer C:** Retelling the story aids comprehension but does not specifically help with making connections to the broader world. **Incorrect Answer:** Creating a timeline is a useful comprehension strategy but does not focus on relating the text to real-world events.
93.	V.	1-D 2-C 3-B 4-A	D. **Fluent.** Conventional spelling. C. **Transitional.** Conventional letters and inventive spelling. B. **Emergent.** Mock handwriting and mock letters. A. **Preliterate.** Random marks or scribbles.

Number	Category	Answer	Explanation
94.	V.	C	**Correct Answer C:** Concepts of print refer to the understanding that print carries meaning, which includes knowing where to start reading on a page, recognizing the directionality of text, and understanding that letters and words are the building blocks of reading. **Incorrect Answer A:** Phonological awareness involves the ability to recognize and manipulate sounds in spoken language, such as rhyming and syllable counting, but it does not pertain to understanding where to start reading in a text. **Incorrect Answer B:** Metacognition refers to the awareness and understanding of one's own thought processes. While important for learning, it is not specifically related to the basic concepts of print. **Incorrect Answer D:** Prosody involves the rhythm, stress, and intonation of speech. While important for fluent reading, it does not address the foundational skill of knowing where to begin reading a text on a page.
95.	V.	A	**Correct Answer A:** Providing students with a robust classroom library where students can self-select books encourages them to engage and interact with various texts, promoting a print-rich environment. **Incorrect Answer B:** While reading aloud to the class is beneficial, it does not actively involve children in interacting with written language on their own, which is crucial in a print-rich environment. **Incorrect Answer C:** Encouraging students to bring books from home is a good practice, but it does not utilize the classroom's print-rich resources as effectively as providing a classroom library does. **Incorrect Answer D:** Displaying students' stories on the bulletin board is positive but does not increase exposure to a print rich environment.
96.	V.	B	**Correct Answer B:** Conducting a "Read Aloud, Think Aloud" session allows the teacher to model the thought processes involved in reading comprehension, helping students become aware of how to monitor and improve their understanding. This is an effective approach to increasing students' metacognition. **Incorrect Answer A:** Assigning daily independent reading time is beneficial but does not explicitly teach or model metacognitive strategies for comprehension. **Incorrect Answer C:** Writing summaries helps with comprehension but does not directly address the metacognitive processes involved in monitoring and improving understanding during reading. **Incorrect Answer D:** Having students read aloud to the class can improve fluency but does not explicitly teach or model metacognitive strategies for comprehension.

Number	Category	Answer	Explanation
97.	V.	A	**Correct Answer A**: A Venn Diagram is the most suitable graphic organizer for comparing and contrasting two subjects, allowing students to visually display similarities and differences between mammals and reptiles. **Incorrect Answer B**: A Timeline is used for displaying events in chronological order and is not effective for comparing and contrasting two subjects. **Incorrect Answer C**: A Concept Map is useful for organizing information about a single concept but is not specifically designed for comparing and contrasting. **Incorrect Answer D**: A Flowchart is best used for showing a sequence of steps or processes, not for comparing and contrasting two subjects.
98.	V.	A	**Correct Answer A**: This question encourages students to connect their personal experiences with the text, making the story more meaningful and memorable for them. **Incorrect Answer B**: While this question asks students to describe Arthur's feelings, it does not prompt them to connect the story to their own lives. **Incorrect Answer C**: This question focuses on making connections with other texts rather than with the students' personal experiences. **Incorrect Answer D**: This question encourages prediction but does not prompt students to relate the text to their own experiences.
99.	V.	C	**Correct Answer C**: Keeping math journals where students write about their problem-solving processes effectively integrates literacy and mathematics. This activity encourages students to articulate their mathematical thinking and use written language to explain their processes, thereby developing their reading and writing skills within the context of math. **Incorrect Answer A**: While sharing feelings about reading in social studies incorporates discussion and reflection, it does not combine reading and writing with other subjects in a structured way that promotes literacy integration. **Incorrect Answer B**: Completing a worksheet with science vocabulary and using the new words in a sentence does integrate literacy with science, but it may not be as engaging or holistic as having students write about their problem-solving processes in math journals. **Incorrect Answer D**: Critiquing art projects is valuable for developing critical thinking and verbal communication skills, but it does not necessarily integrate reading and writing in the context of other academic subjects.

Number	Category	Answer	Explanation
100.	V.	D	**Correct Answer D**: Discussing how the story changes when told from the wolf's perspective compared to the traditional version helps students understand the concept of point of view. This activity highlights how different narrators can influence the interpretation of a story. **Incorrect Answer A**: Drawing a favorite scene from the story engages students in visualizing the story but does not specifically address understanding point of view. **Incorrect Answer B**: Acting out the story as it was originally written can be a fun activity but does not help students compare different points of view. **Incorrect Answer C**: Writing a summary of the story helps with comprehension but does not specifically focus on understanding how point of view affects storytelling.
101.	V.	C	**Correct Answer C:** Subitizing is the ability to recognize the number of objects in a small group without needing to count them individually. **Incorrect Answer A:** Transitivity refers to a logical relationship. For example, if A is larger than B, and B is larger than C, then A is larger than C. **Incorrect Answer B:** Patterns involve recognizing and predicting sequences or arrangements based on repeating or consistent elements. **Incorrect Answer D:** Decomposition refers to breaking down a complex problem or object into smaller, more manageable parts.
102.	V.	B	Answer B is the only choice out of the 4 options that shows a pattern.
103.	V.	C	**Correct Answer C:** Before students can classify and categorize geometric shapes, they need to recognize and understand the attributes of these shapes, such as the number of sides, angles, and vertices. This foundational knowledge is essential for any further work with shapes. **Incorrect Answer A:** Defining area is a more advanced concept that involves understanding measurement and space. It is not a prerequisite for classifying and categorizing geometric shapes based on their attributes. **Incorrect Answer B:** While drawing shapes can help students become familiar with different shapes, the skill of recognizing shape attributes is more directly related to the objective of classifying and categorizing shapes. **Incorrect Answer D:** Identifying patterns is a valuable skill in mathematics but is not specifically related to the prerequisite knowledge needed for classifying and categorizing geometric shapes based on their attributes.

Number	Category	Answer	Explanation
104.	V.	A	Using nonstandard units of measure means using something other than a ruler or tape measure to measure objects. Students measuring desks with paperclips or pencils is a common early childhood practice of using nonstandard units of measure.
105.	V.	C	In this case, students are organizing data. They are putting all the different animals in order and organizing it in a way that they can see how many students like which animal. Organizing data is an essential early skill in math.
106.	V.	A	This is a fraction strip representing $\frac{1}{2}$.
107.	V.	B	The phrase *how many more* in the question stem indicates subtraction. You must subtract Sidney's pieces from Jan's pieces, and you get a difference of 3 pieces.
108.	V.	D	Place value is determining the number value of an underlined part of a multidigit number. In this case, the place value is 40 because the 4 is in the 10s place.
109.	V.	D	In this case 25% and $\frac{1}{4}$ of the squares represent the same fraction in different ways.
110.	V.	D	**Correct Answer D**: Pie charts or circle graphs are most effective in displaying percentages. The entire pie or circle represents 100%. Then each slice represents the pieces or percentages. This pie chart or circle graph would look like this: ■ Strawberry ▨ Vanilla ▨ Chocolate **Incorrect Answer A**: A line graph is best used for showing data changes over time, not for displaying percentages of a whole. **Incorrect Answer B**: While a bar graph can represent data, it is more suited for comparing different categories or values rather than showing parts of a whole, such as percentages. **Incorrect Answer C**: A pictograph uses pictures to represent data and can be useful for simple comparisons but is not as effective as a circle graph for showing percentages of a whole.

Number	Category	Answer	Explanation
111.	V.	C	**Correct Answer C:** The concrete approach involves using physical objects or manipulatives, such as snap cubes, to help students understand mathematical concepts. This hands-on method allows students to visualize and physically manipulate items to solve addition problems, building a strong foundation for abstract thinking. **Incorrect Answer A:** The abstract approach involves using symbols and numbers without the support of physical objects or visual aids. This method is more advanced and relies on students' ability to conceptualize mathematical operations mentally. **Incorrect Answer B:** Fluency in math refers to the ability to solve problems accurately and quickly, often involving practice and repetition to achieve automaticity. While fluency is an important skill, it does not describe the use of snap cubes in this context. **Incorrect Answer D:** The representational approach, also known as the pictorial stage, involves using drawings or visual models to represent mathematical concepts. Although it bridges the gap between concrete and abstract stages, it does not involve the direct use of physical objects like snap cubes.
112.	V.	A	**Correct Answer A:** Using dot paper or a geoboard is an effective strategy for young students to explore and understand the attributes of two-dimensional figures. This hands-on approach allows students to manipulate shapes and observe their characteristics in an interactive and engaging way, which is appropriate for their developmental level. **Incorrect Answer B:** While making a table to list attributes can be useful, it is more abstract and may not be as effective for kindergarten students who benefit more from hands-on, visual activities at the beginning of their learning process. **Incorrect Answer C:** Using geometric formulas is too advanced for kindergarten students. At this stage, students are just beginning to learn about basic shapes and their attributes through concrete experiences rather than abstract formulas. **Incorrect Answer D:** Base ten blocks are typically used for teaching place value and other numerical concepts. They are not the best tool for exploring the attributes of two-dimensional figures, which require more specific geometric manipulatives.
113.	V.	A	The concrete representation of the multiplication problem 3 x 5 is a picture or array of 3 groups of 5 items. The array in option A contains 3 rows, each with 5 dots.

Number	Category	Answer	Explanation
114.	V.	A	**Correct Answer A**: Counting and Cardinality – This activity primarily focuses on helping students count and compare quantities, which falls under the concept of counting and cardinality. **Incorrect Answer B**: Addition and Subtraction – Although students are identifying totals, the primary focus of the activity is on counting and comparing quantities, not performing addition or subtraction operations. **Incorrect Answer C**: Measurement and Data – While measurement and data involve organizing and interpreting data, this activity is more centered on counting and comparing specific quantities. **Incorrect Answer D**: Geometry – This activity does not involve shapes, spatial reasoning, or other geometric concepts.
115.	V.	C	**Correct Answer C**: Conservation of numbers – This activity is designed to help students understand that the number of objects remains the same even when rearranged, which is the concept of conservation of numbers. **Incorrect Answer A**: Pattern recognition – While recognizing patterns is an important mathematical skill, this activity is focused on understanding that the quantity of objects does not change with their arrangement. **Incorrect Answer B**: Spatial reasoning – Although spatial reasoning involves understanding shapes and spaces, this activity is primarily about recognizing the consistent quantity of objects despite changes in arrangement. **Incorrect Answer D**: Addition and subtraction – This activity does not involve performing operations of addition or subtraction but is about understanding the consistent count of objects.
116.	V.	D	**Correct Answer D**: Flexibility – Mr. Thompson should focus on improving the students' ability to choose and explain different strategies for arriving at a correct answer, which relates to their deep understanding of math concepts, not just speed or recall. **Incorrect Answer A**: Accuracy – While accuracy is important, it refers to solving problems using the correct method and arriving at the correct answer, which these students already achieve. **Incorrect Answer B**: Automaticity – Automaticity involves providing a correct answer as an automatic response, which is not the issue in this scenario. **Incorrect Answer C**: Rate – The rate relates to the quick recall of a math fact, but Mr. Thompson is concerned with the students' ability to explain their methods, not their speed.

Number	Category	Answer	Explanation
117.	V.	C	**Correct Answer C**: Rate – Ms. Wilson is focusing on the speed and accuracy of her students' responses, which corresponds to the rate aspect of math fact fluency. **Incorrect Answer A**: Accuracy – Although accuracy is a part of the assessment, the focus on speed indicates that the primary concern is the rate. **Incorrect Answer B**: Automaticity – Automaticity involves efficient strategies for finding the correct answer, but the primary focus here is on the speed of recall. **Incorrect Answer D**: Flexibility – Flexibility involves choosing and explaining different strategies for arriving at a correct answer, which is not the primary focus in this assessment of speed and accuracy.
118.	V.	B	**Correct Answer B**: Counting a mixed set of blocks that vary in color, shape, and size demonstrates the concept of abstraction because it shows that the quantity of items remains the same regardless of their physical characteristics. **Incorrect Answer A**: Counting identical red blocks does not fully illustrate abstraction, as it does not involve variations in characteristics. **Incorrect Answer C**: Counting by twos using a number line focuses on skip counting, not abstraction. **Incorrect Answer D**: Reciting numbers from 1 to 20 focuses on rote memorization, not the abstraction principle in counting.
119.	V.	D	**Correct Answer D**: Compensation is the strategy Ms. Green is teaching. By rounding 9 up to 10 and then adjusting by subtracting 1, students can simplify the addition process. **Incorrect Answer A**: Subitizing is the ability to instantly recognize the number of objects in a small group without counting. This strategy does not involve adjusting numbers to make calculations easier. **Incorrect Answer B**: One-to-one correspondence is the understanding that each object being counted represents one unit. This concept is fundamental to counting but is not related to adjusting numbers for easier addition. **Incorrect Answer C**: Pattern identification involves recognizing and using patterns to understand mathematical concepts. While useful, it is not the strategy described in this scenario for simplifying addition.

Practice Test 1

Number	Category	Answer	Explanation
120.	V.	D	**Correct Answer D:** Using a number line - This strategy can effectively help students visualize subtraction by allowing them to start at a given number and move left to find the difference.
			Incorrect Answer A: Subitizing - This refers to instantly recognizing the number of objects without counting, which is not relevant to the subtraction process being described.
			Incorrect Answer B: Compensation - This strategy involves adjusting numbers to make calculations easier, which is not being used in this context where the teacher is focusing on subtraction.
			Incorrect Answer C: One-to-one correspondence - This involves matching one object to one number or item to ensure each object is counted once, which does not directly apply to visualizing subtraction with a number line.

This page intentionally left blank.

Good Words List

The following list of words and phrases will help you *Think Like a Test Maker*™ and locate correct and eliminate bad answer choices. When you work backward from the answer choices, you identify answers containing good words, eliminate those with bad words, and then read the question.

Good Words

Understanding the *Good Words List* is essential for supporting young children's development and learning. These terms reflect best practices in early childhood education, focusing on engaging, inclusive, and developmentally appropriate methods that cater to individual needs and promote holistic growth.

Attachment Theory – A psychological model describing the dynamics of long-term relationships between humans, particularly focusing on the bonds between children and their caregivers.

Autonomy – The ability to make one's own decisions and act independently. In early childhood education, promoting autonomy helps children develop self-confidence and decision-making skills.

Conflict Resolution – Strategies and methods used to resolve disagreements and disputes. Effective conflict resolution helps children learn to handle conflicts constructively and build positive relationships.

Constructivism – An educational theory that emphasizes the role of learners in constructing their own understanding and knowledge through experiences and interactions. Constructivism supports active learning and problem-solving.

Curiosity – A strong desire to learn or know more about something. Encouraging curiosity fosters a love for learning and exploration in young children.

Developmentally Appropriate Practices (DAP) – Educational practices that are based on how children develop and learn best. DAP involves tailoring teaching strategies to match the developmental stages and individual needs of children.

Differentiation – The process of tailoring instruction to meet the diverse needs of students. Differentiation involves adjusting content, processes, products, and learning environments to ensure all students can achieve success.

Early Intervention – The process of providing specialized services and support to young children who are at risk for or show signs of developmental delays or disabilities. Early intervention aims to address challenges and promote optimal development.

Emotional Intelligence – The ability to recognize, understand, and manage one's own emotions, as well as recognize, understand, and influence the emotions of others. Emotional intelligence is crucial for building strong relationships and effective communication.

Empathy – The ability to understand and share the feelings of another person. Teaching and modeling empathy helps children develop strong interpersonal skills and supportive relationships.

Formative Assessment – Assessments conducted during the learning process to monitor student progress and inform instruction. Formative assessments help educators adjust teaching strategies to better meet the needs of students.

Inclusion – The practice of integrating all children, including those with disabilities, into regular educational settings. Inclusion ensures that every child has access to the same learning opportunities and social interactions.

Individualized Instruction – Tailoring teaching methods and learning activities to meet the unique needs and abilities of each student. Individualized instruction ensures that all learners receive appropriate support to succeed.

Inquiry – A process of seeking information and answers through exploration and questioning. Inquiry-based learning helps children develop critical thinking and problem-solving skills.

Multisensory Learning – An instructional approach that engages more than one sense at a time (e.g., sight, sound, touch) to enhance learning and memory. Multisensory learning helps cater to different learning styles and needs.

Play – Engaging in activities for enjoyment and recreation. Play is crucial for children's social, emotional, cognitive, and physical development.

Positive Behavior Supports – Strategies and interventions designed to promote positive behavior and reduce challenging behavior. This approach helps create a supportive learning environment.

Practiced Routines and Procedures – Established and regularly followed methods and activities help create a structured and predictable classroom environment. Practiced routines and procedures enhance classroom management and help students understand expectations.

Responsive Teaching – Adapting teaching practices based on students' needs, interests, and feedback. Responsive teaching promotes a dynamic and flexible learning environment that meets the diverse needs of all students.

Scaffolding – Providing support and guidance to help children achieve tasks they cannot complete independently. Scaffolding involves gradually removing support as children gain more skills and confidence.

Self-efficacy – The belief in one's own ability to succeed in specific situations. Developing self-efficacy helps children take on challenges and persist through difficulties.

Self-regulation – The ability to control one's emotions, thoughts, and behaviors in different situations. Self-regulation is important for managing impulses and interacting appropriately with others.

Social-Emotional Learning – The process of developing skills to understand and manage emotions, set and achieve positive goals, feel and show empathy for others, establish and maintain positive relationships, and make responsible decisions.

Targeted Interventions – Specific strategies and supports designed to address the needs of individual students who require additional help.

Universal Design for Learning (UDL) – An educational framework that aims to optimize teaching and learning for all individuals by providing multiple means of representation, engagement, and action/expression. UDL ensures that instruction is accessible and effective for diverse learners.

Mastering these terms is crucial for both success on the Praxis Education of Young Children Exam and effective practice in the classroom. Here's why:

- **Effective Instruction:** Concepts like differentiation and targeted interventions are essential for addressing diverse learning needs and ensuring that all students receive appropriate support and challenges.

- **Holistic Development:** Terms such as emotional intelligence, social-emotional learning, and scaffolding contribute to a comprehensive approach to fostering students' emotional, social, and cognitive growth.

- **Inclusive Practices:** Understanding inclusion and Universal Design for Learning (UDL) helps educators create environments that support the learning of all students, regardless of their abilities or backgrounds.

- **Engaging Learning Environments:** Encouraging curiosity, play, and inquiry promotes an engaging and interactive learning environment, helping to maintain students' motivation and interest.

- **Ongoing Assessment and Adaptation:** Knowing how to use formative assessment and responsive teaching allows educators to continuously monitor and adapt their instruction to meet the evolving needs of their students.

Bad Words

Recognizing the terms in the Bad Words List helps educators avoid less effective or counterproductive practices. These practices may fail to address diverse learning needs, create stress, or foster a negative learning environment. By avoiding these practices, educators can focus on creating supportive, effective, and engaging learning experiences that enhance student success and well-being.

Extra Homework – While it may seem like a way to reinforce learning, excessive or inappropriate extra homework can lead to stress and a lack of balance in students' lives.

Multiple Choice Tests – While they can test certain types of knowledge, multiple-choice tests may not accurately measure a student's deeper understanding or critical thinking skills.

One-Size-Fits-All Approach – This approach can be ineffective as it does not accommodate the diverse learning styles and developmental stages of students.

Punitive Measures – Discipline strategies that use punishment or negative consequences to manage behavior can create a negative learning environment and may not address the underlying causes of behavioral issues.

Relying on Outside Help – Relying heavily on outside help can undermine the effectiveness of classroom teaching and may not address the root causes of learning challenges.

Worksheets – Worksheets can be a passive form of learning and may not always engage students in meaningful or hands-on experiences that promote deeper understanding.

Recognizing why these terms represent less effective or inappropriate practices is crucial for success on the Praxis Education of Young Children Exam and for effective teaching. Here's why:

- **Focus on Engagement:** Terms like *worksheets* and *multiple-choice tests* often fail to engage students in meaningful learning experiences. Understanding these limitations helps educators seek more dynamic and interactive approaches that foster deeper learning and student engagement.

- **Supportive Strategies:** Relying on outside help and a one-size-fits-all approach may not address the diverse needs of all students. Recognizing these pitfalls encourages educators to use differentiation and targeted interventions to meet individual needs within the classroom better.

- **Positive Learning Environment:** Extra homework and punitive measures can contribute to stress and a negative learning environment. Understanding these drawbacks highlights the importance of creating a balanced and supportive environment that promotes positive behavior and student well-being.

- **Effective Assessment:** While useful for certain assessments, multiple-choice tests may not provide a complete picture of student understanding. This awareness helps educators explore various assessment methods, including formative assessment, to better gauge and support student learning.

This page intentionally left blank.

Bibliography

Bandura, A. (1997). *Self-Efficacy: The Exercise of Control.* New York, NY: W. H. Freeman and Company.

Bruner, J. S. (1960). *The Process of Education.* Cambridge, MA: Harvard University Press.

CAST (Center for Applied Special Technology). (2018). *Universal Design for Learning: Theory and Practice.* Retrieved from https://www.cast.org/impact/universal-design-for-learning-udl

Common Core State Standards Initiative. (2010). *Common Core State Standards for English Language Arts and Literacy in History/Social Studies, Science, and Technical Subjects.* Washington, DC: National Governors Association Center for Best Practices, Council of Chief State School Officers.

Constructivist Learning Theory. (1999). *The Museum and the Needs of People.* John H. Falk and Lynn D. Dierking (Eds.). Retrieved from https://www.exploratorium.edu/education/ifi/constructivist-learning

Council for Exceptional Children (CEC). (2014). *Standards for Evidence-Based Practices in Special Education.* Arlington, VA: CEC.

Gardner, H. (1983). *Frames of Mind: The Theory of Multiple Intelligences.* New York, NY: Basic Books.

Maslow, A. H. (1943). *A Theory of Human Motivation.* Psychological Review, 50(4), 370-396.

Multi-Tiered System of Supports (MTSS). (2020). *MTSS in Action: What it Looks Like in Elementary Schools.* Retrieved from https://www.mtss4success.org/

National Association for the Education of Young Children (NAEYC). (2009). *Standards for Early Childhood Professional Preparation.* Washington, DC: NAEYC.

Piaget, J. (1952). *The Origins of Intelligence in Children.* New York, NY: International Universities Press.

Tomlinson, C. A. (2001). *How to Differentiate Instruction in Mixed-Ability Classrooms.* Alexandria, VA: Association for Supervision and Curriculum Development.

Universal Design for Learning (UDL). (2018). *UDL Guidelines.* Retrieved from https://udlguidelines.cast.org/

Vygotsky, L. S. (1978). *Mind in Society: The Development of Higher Psychological Processes.* Cambridge, MA: Harvard University Press.

Bibliography

Made in the USA
Las Vegas, NV
19 September 2024

95515860R00109